AUTHOR PRENEUR

JESSE WARREN TEVELOW

LT PRESS

Authorpreneur / Jesse Warren Tevelow
First Edition: 2018
Printed in the United States of America
Design by The Frontispiece and Jesse Tevelow

1. Lifestyle. 2. Entrepreneurship. 3. Writing.
 I. Title: Authorpreneur
ISBN 978-1982055554

For My Dad

CONTENTS

GET YOUR FREE RESOURCES

A comprehensive package of exclusive resources come with this book as a free bonus. There's also a free online course designed to provide additional guidance. To be sure you get the most out of the *Authorpreneur* experience, download all the extras and access the companion course at the link below:

http://www.jtev.me/authorpreneur-free-course

GET THE AUDIOBOOK FOR FREE

I've recorded this entire book on audio for your convenience, and you can listen to it for free. Visit the link below to get the audio version:

http://www.jtev.me/authorpreneur-audio-version

"You, sitting in your apartment, can communicate with everyone on Earth more effectively than any media company twenty years ago."

— TAYLOR PEARSON, *The End of Jobs*

"You will be the greatest generation. When we look back 50 years from now, 100 years from now, 500 years from now, you will be the generation that unlocked human potential."

—BEN HOROWITZ, *Columbia University Commencement Speech*

AUTHORPRENEUR

NEUROSURGEONS, BESTSELLERS, AND BAGS OF CASH

After a night of broken sleep, I was groggy and stressed. Wearing nothing but a pair of boxers, I sunk my teeth into an apple and sat down in front of my computer. I nudged my mouse to wake the screen from its sleep mode, and there it was: a long-winded email from a complete stranger that would alter the course of my life.

Jesse,

Thanks for providing the details on how to get started with blogging, something I've wanted to do for some time—both medical and life philosophy stuff. And also thanks for validating my desire to write a book or two (even if I am the only reader).

There are many fascinating things that I have done (and many more I plan to do), both professionally and personally, that have really influenced my view of the world. I've seen the best in people, and the worst in people. I've had great teachers and mentors, and very bad ones. I have rejoiced with my patients and families at their highest points in life: the births of sons and daughters, or a miraculous recovery from a life-threatening event. And I have been to the depths of human emotion, weeping with families when they are saying goodbye to their children with brain tumors or other horrible affliction.

I have seen just about every way that adults can destroy their bodies and souls; and how bravely children always fight to get well, so that they can get back to school with their friends and play ball. Life is full of incredible juxtapositions...

So true. Full of juxtapositions. Todd was an accomplished neurosurgeon from Florida and he had just

PART ONE

THE POWER OF THE WRITTEN WORD

CHAPTER 1

WELCOME TO THE WRITER REVOLUTION

The Seven-Figure Side Gig

Have you ever felt frustrated with your career, or that you're somehow selling yourself short? Ever wished you could harness your passion and find financial freedom in the process? I know I have. But for most of us, that's as far as it goes. The thought evaporates as quickly as it forms. It's a half-hearted prayer, an unattainable goal whispered aimlessly into the night, *a dream*. Eventually, we wake up from our fantasy and go back to reality.

Miraculously, at the not-so-ripe age of 31, I found myself in the position to chase the dream with my eyes open. I had just been fired from my first startup, and I had precisely zero plans for my future. With enough savings in the bank to survive for about a year, I hunkered down in my one-bedroom apartment and started writing.

Less than eighteen months later, I had two #1 best-sellers on Amazon and I was earning thousands of dollars per month in passive income. I had seen the light: Writing can be a viable side-gig, a powerful leveraging tool, and even a lucrative full-time pursuit. It can open doors you never knew existed. But perhaps most importantly, it can bring you more fulfillment than you've ever felt before. That's exactly what it did for me.

According to a *New York Times* article, four out of every five Americans feel the urge to write a book,[1] yet very few of us (less than one percent) actually go through with it. Why? Because writing a book has historically been categorized as an impossible task. It's like winning the lottery. First you have to write a mind-blowing story. Then you have to hire an agent. Then you have to score a publishing deal. And even if you somehow pull that off, it'll take years before your book hits the shelves. *"Writing a book is a fool's game."*

---

1 https://tinyurl.com/25w5cy7

This is the story we've been told, and it was accurate until about 2007. But a lot has changed since then, and society hasn't caught up yet. Years into the future, we'll have a new set of fools: Those who continued believing the same old story.

I wrote my first book in six months, making countless mistakes along the way. I didn't have a publisher, or an editor, or an email list, or a marketing team, yet I still managed to publish a #1 bestseller that generates significant income. I then leveraged that success into a powerful brand and business. The experience blew my mind, to put it lightly. I couldn't help but wonder, *"Are other people seeing the same results?"* As I dug deeper, I found multiple examples 0f indie authors making five, six, and sometimes even *seven* figures from their self-published books and related companies. And then it hit me: *We now live in a world that favors content creators over gatekeepers.*

Here's the deal: If you're entrepreneurial and hardworking, you can use books to earn meaningful passive income, gain leverage as an expert in your field, build your legacy, grow a sustainable business, and enrich the world. And you don't need anyone's permission. You can just do it. I know it sounds hyperbolic and crazy, but it's true. This is the most favorable environment for writing books the world has ever seen. By the time you're done reading this, I want you to understand two things:

1. How technology and entrepreneurship have made books more powerful than ever before
2. How to "profit" from this unique opportunity (in every sense of the word)

Now, right now—meaning *today,* is the best time to start writing, and you'll find out *why* in the pages that follow. If you already agree with me, you can skip ahead, although you might find the explanation interesting and inspiring.[2]

After laying out the *why,* I'll show you *how*. I'll explain how I wrote *The Connection Algorithm,* how it got ranked within the top 0.1% of all books on the Kindle platform, and how I achieved a $20,000-per-year passive income stream directly from launch (with no pre-existing brand and no email list). I'll also tell you how I wrote my second book, *Hustle,* in the span of seven days (and still hit #1 in multiple categories on Amazon). And finally, I'll show you how I leveraged my books (including this one) to build a thriving business.

Throughout the book, we'll also examine other self-published authors whose titles are performing far better than mine. Some of them are earning

---

2   Tactical information for writing, launching, and selling your book starts at Part Two. If that's your focus, feel free to skip all the philosophical stuff (Part One).

hundreds of thousands—or even *millions* of dollars. Many of them have morphed their writing careers into multimillion-dollar ventures. Others started off with a business and amplified it with a book. This isn't theory. These are real-world examples. I've interviewed dozens of these inspiring trailblazers, who I've aptly nicknamed "authorpreneurs," to get firsthand accounts of their success. I've also worked with many of them directly through my company.

After reading this book, you'll have the courage to explore the authorpreneur lifestyle for yourself, along with the knowledge to execute it. You don't need a huge following. You don't need a bankroll. And you don't need to be an expert. You just need to get started.

This Book is NOT for Authors

Let me set the record straight. If you want to become the next J.K. Rowling, you're in the wrong place. This book is actually *not* for aspiring authors (in the traditional sense). It's for anyone seeking more freedom, purpose, and wealth. Whether you're a CEO, an entrepreneur, a blue-collar worker, a student, a recent grad, or a stay-at-home mom or dad—publishing a book will enhance your life. The broad effects of writing, publishing, and marketing books are complementary to *any* project, product, or business. So this is more than just a writing guide. It's a blueprint for living a more prosperous life and thriving in the entrepreneurial era. (More on that later).

From the stories found in the following pages, you'll see how entrepreneurs are using books to start businesses, build powerful relationships, and establish credibility in their fields. Writing lets you gain leverage *everywhere*. Long story short: If you're *not* J.K. Rowling, this book is most certainly for you.

How to Read this Book

We're taught to go from start to finish—from A to Z. Grade school, high school, college, grad school. Job, spouse, house, kids. "Don't get up until your plate is cleared. Finish your chores. *Finish the book*." Well, you have my permission to forget these rules. You don't need to read this book from cover to cover. You can jump around. If a particular section doesn't seem relevant to you, hop back to the table of contents and look for something that catches your eye.

I've deliberately separated the book into two main parts. The first part is philosophical. It explains the *why* behind writing a book, detailing the many ways in which it can change your life. The second part is tactical. It explains the *how:* How to write well, market effectively, and optimize your results. If you already understand the benefits of writing and just want to learn how to leverage your book successfully, skip ahead to part two.

What's in it For You?

The democratization of production and distribution afforded by the internet is a double-edged sword. While it provides tremendous opportunity to a much broader swath of society, it also creates a crapload of noise. Google *"how to publish a book"* and you'll find a dense spiderweb of fragmented, lousy, and down-right *incorrect* information. That's because publishing a book isn't easy.

Lucky for you, I've been through the entire process and experienced a high degree of success. In fact, my company performs strategic book launches for people just like you, and we've perfected our systems over time. I've even taken it a step further by conducting interviews with respected experts, including publishers, marketers, and #1 bestselling authors. So I'm here to give you everything you need in one complete package. This is your central, trusted source.

My goal is to help you get rich from writing. I'll unpack that statement later, because there's a lot to unpack. If you're reading this, I assume you have an interest in either writing or entrepreneurship. But I want to show you how the two intersect, and how people are already profiting from that intersection. Hence the title, *Authorpreneur.*

Note: There's a comprehensive package of exclusive resources that come with this book as a bonus. There's also a free online course designed to provide additional guidance. To be sure you get the most out of the Authorpreneur experience, download the extras and access the companion course at the link below:

www.jtev.me/authorpreneur-free-course

CHAPTER 2

THE ARGUMENT FOR WRITING A BOOK

The market for writing books, particularly digital books, has never been better for new authors. But there are also timeless benefits to writing that have been lost or forgotten in our modern culture. After reading this section, you'll feel more confident about the power of writing, and understand why *now* is the best time to jump in. To fully grasp why books have become such an effective tool for personal growth, we must first examine the new driving force in our economy: *entrepreneurship*.

Why Writing a Book Is the New PhD

There's a big problem brewing. People all over the country (and the world), are finally starting to realize it: *At the core, universities are no longer higher-learning institutions. First and foremost, they're businesses.*

This means they want to bring as many students through their doors as possible. For centuries, they've quietly whispered their battle cry into our ears: *"You must attend college to succeed."* It's a brilliant marketing message, and it works. Affluent people tend to obey the command. In fact, it's been so ingrained in our culture that our parents reinforced the unwritten rule when we were growing up. If you were like me, you went to college and accumulated debt because it was branded as the common-sense choice. (*"It's the only way to get ahead! It'll pay off later!"*)

I'm sure you know what comes next. Immediately after tossing your graduation cap into the air, the real world punched you in the face. You quickly came to realize that your shiny, framed degree was practically worthless. It's a commodity. It's *expected*. Fast forward to today. Now you're in debt, but you have no competitive advantage. You're screwed, like everyone else. Go sit in your cubicle and shuffle papers until it's time to head home. Eventually you'll get promoted (maybe).

Yes, this situation sucks. You might even feel like it's unacceptable. Is there a way out? How can you gain leverage? How can you differentiate yourself? More importantly, how can you live a life of purpose? Don't worry, if you look hard enough, there's always a solution—and you've already found it.

> **Giving yourself an edge requires playing a different game. Writing books is the new differentiator.**

Simply put, writing books is no longer just for authors. It's for anyone who wants to gain upward mobility. And it's for anyone who has something worth saying, or teaching—which is everyone. Power is rapidly shifting from the corporation to the individual, but it won't be handed to you on a silver platter. You have to *seize* it.

The traditional path of the past century is no longer stable. A college degree isn't a ticket that grants us access to ascend the corporate ladder. Because jobs as we currently understand them are increasingly being managed by machines or shipped overseas, companies are downsizing their staffs, leaving only the core members who make the organization run. And even if you're among those workers, the heightened competition for such roles means employers are more likely to drop you for someone more qualified or less expensive. There's no security and no stability. Working for a corporation has become risky.

To make matters worse, *knowledge itself* is now a commodity too, just like a college degree. The internet allows us to query basic information, so memorizing facts and figures is no longer valuable. Today, the power lies in whatever *can't* be easily queried—things like: "Which problem should we solve next?" or "How can we make this experience better than the existing one?" These are entrepreneurial questions.

Those of us willing to explore entrepreneurship are realizing it's becoming the *safer* path. Working in an institution isn't necessarily bad. We just need to realize that job security is a thing of the past. By definition, an entrepreneur can adapt and thrive in rapidly changing environments, so familiarizing yourself with those behaviors is the smartest strategy for long-term success, whether you plan to freelance, start your own business, or work for a bigger organization.

To be clear, I'm not suggesting everyone should become a startup founder and build a billion-dollar business. I'm saying everyone should develop entrepreneurial skills. Advanced problem-solving, decision-making, creativity, and content-creation will be the most valuable disciplines in the workplaces of tomorrow.

As logic-based tasks become largely software operated, companies are seeking people who excel in the *creative and complex* realms. They're valuing entrepreneurs over all other workers. The term "acqu-hire" has bubbled up into the business lexicon to describe very small companies being bought by bigger companies, purely for talent (vs. product). Companies like Google and Facebook use this strategy to bring teams of 1-10 people onboard, paying millions of dollars to acquire new employees with entrepreneurial backgrounds.

To bring this all into focus, you need to realize that **writing a book happens to be one of the best ways to develop entrepreneurial skills.** By publishing a nonfiction (lifestyle, technical, or philosophical) book, you're experiencing entrepreneurship in two profound ways:

1. Self-learning is one of the most basic tenets of being an entrepreneur. Nonfiction books serve that need, so you're feeding the most important growing audience in our culture.
2. By writing and publishing a book, you're developing your own entrepreneurial skills, while simultaneously establishing yourself as an expert in whatever you're writing about.

Being a published author is the bargaining chip your college education failed to deliver. And the act of writing, publishing, and marketing your book is arguably the best training program for excelling in the entrepreneurial economy. James Altucher championed this belief in *Choose Yourself,* which was coincidentally one of the first self-published bestsellers on Amazon, with hundreds of thousands of copies sold. He said, "self-publishing is the new business card."[1] I'll take it a step further: *Self-publishing is the new PhD.*

There are five main reasons why writing is one of the easiest ways to get started along the path of entrepreneurship*:*

1. *Writing and publishing a book is exactly like running a startup.* (I should know. I've done both). When you write a book, you're creating a product from nothing. Then you're distributing and marketing it. Then you're analyzing and optimizing its sales. This is the full product lifecycle every startup endures.

2. *Publishing a book requires almost no capital.* There is now a robust infrastructure in place for you to go from concept to launch with *very little* upfront cost (a few thousand dollars, at most).

---

1 https://tinyurl.com/m2u5ao7

3. *You don't need any skills except the knowledge you already possess.* There are a lot of sexy ways to generate income these days: Build an app, host a podcast, launch an ecommerce store, create a YouTube channel, etc. Those are all viable approaches, but writing a book is still the easiest way to start, by far. The learning curve to build apps or launch a podcast is much steeper than becoming a good writer, mainly because we're all taught how to write from a very young age. Writing just hasn't ever been as lucrative as it is today.

4. *It's flexible.* You can do this while keeping your current job. You can probably even make progress *at* your job. For the same reason mentioned above, writing is extremely accessible. You don't need any complicated software or tools to get started. It's impossible to record a podcast at your desk at work, but you can easily chip away at your book.

5. *It's infinitely applicable.* Because of a phenomenon known as *The Long Tail*,[2] even the most obscure topics are now profitable. Later, we'll

---

2 https://tinyurl.com/nppk4kk

see examples of authors making serious cash from very specific subject matters. This is possible because of the unparalleled accessibility of products in an internet-connected world. Twenty years ago, it would have been impossible to find everyone on the planet who liked making sweaters for cats. So if you wrote a book about cat sweaters, you wouldn't sell enough copies to earn meaningful income. There was a discovery and distribution problem. Today, those niche audiences can be accurately targeted on the internet with a few clicks.

As the college diploma becomes the new high school diploma—and all the world's information is compiled into a single, searchable index in our pockets—differentiating ourselves is becoming a challenge. We need a new approach. Entrepreneurship is the next phase of our economy, and publishing a book is a highly entrepreneurial endeavor with almost no barriers to entry. This isn't just about writing a book. It's bigger than that. It's about flexing your entrepreneurial muscles and understanding your limitless power in a world without walls. If you want an unfair advantage in business and in life, it's time to start writing.

The Library in Your Hand

The accessibility of knowledge today would be unimaginable to previous generations. And the actual *speed* of learning is conservatively 1,000 times faster than it has ever been. As famed investor Ben Horowitz explains: In the past, "looking stuff up was very discouraging because you couldn't look it up in milliseconds. It took *hours,* and that's if you were a Columbia student and you had a good library."[3]

While the internet makes learning faster, it still presents challenges. The endless influx of content can be deafening and distracting. And without any formal curation system, the quality of information is often lacking. But that's okay. The freedom of the internet means it's also self-correcting. *Access to experts* is one of the most compelling emerging solutions.

The Virtual Classroom: Expert Access

For a price, we can now learn directly from experts online. This new channel for deep learning is cheaper, more accessible, and more actionable than traditional education. Here are three examples:

Udemy

Udemy (pronounced "you-to-me") is a platform for

---

3 https://tinyurl.com/y7vp7v2w

"Everybody who has a smartphone, which is pretty soon going to be everybody in the world, has the Library of Congress in their pocket. So that means a girl growing up in Bangladesh now, has a better library than a student at Columbia or Harvard had twenty years ago." [†]

—BEN HOROWITZ

[†] https://tinyurl.com/y7vp7v2w

learning anything. Anyone can be an instructor, and anyone can be a student. Instructors create courses by uploading videos and offering other downloadable materials for their course. Anyone can then pay for the course and consume it online at their own pace.

Teachable
Teachable is similar to Udemy. I used Teachable to offer the companion course to this book, and it's completely free. You can check it out here:

www.jtev.me/authorepreneur-free-course

Thinkific
Thinkific is another similar option where you can create and consume curated online courses.

Many of the experts on these platforms, like Seth Godin, are professionals in their field who are succeeding *right now*. Would you rather learn from the expert excelling in the field, or the professor regurgitating outdated theories from a textbook? (Do they still use actual textbooks?)

This is just the beginning of the online learning revolution. So, regardless of the topic you're writing about, you can access quality content and become an expert with relative ease. Authors previously paid thousands of dollars to meet with professors, or listen to experts give seminars, or interview industry experts. Now we can take comprehensive courses from the comfort of own homes and on our own time, for a fraction of the cost.[4]

The Long Tail: Market Fragmentation

It's natural to experience our reality through the lens of corporate America and academia. Those institutions tell us to study business, economics, literature, science, math, and history. All of those disciplines are certainly useful, but they aren't all-encompassing. In reality, the world values knowledge in absolutely *anything*. This doesn't just apply to books.

Here's one example, taken from my first book, *The Connection Algorithm*: Playing video games. New businesses are cropping up, like Twitch,[5] which streams live online video of gamers playing their favorite games. Tournaments have sprouted up around the globe, bringing together the most competitive and skilled gamers on the planet. These professional

---

4 Yes, some of the courses offered on these platforms can be lacking in quality. But that's okay. Overall, there's an abundance of valuable information that was completely unavailable twenty years ago. And typically, the best stuff rises to the top, spreading through word-of-mouth.
5 http://www.twitch.tv/

gamers are earning serious income, some making hundreds of thousands of dollars a year.[6]

To those of us who play games as a hobby, this seems ridiculous. But these professional gamers are able to fund their lives by playing video games because *they're extremely good at it*. It's taken me half a lifetime to realize that any talent can generate income. V*alue* is the key ingredient. In the context of writing a book, this means you can literally write about *anything*. The only criteria is that other people find it useful.

This wouldn't have worked twenty years ago. It works today because of the Long Tail. The scope of your knowledge, even if it's limited to a specific domain, is monetizable. Don't wait until you're an expert to write your book. Write your book now to *become* the expert. Using the library in your hand and the unparalleled access to experts online, *anyone* can create compelling content.

Books Make You Rich

Being a published author feels great, but most of us want more than that. We eventually expect remuneration—i.e. money! We all want to be rich, but what does that really mean? A long time ago, I cofounded my first company. There were millions of dollars flowing into

_____

6 https://tinyurl.com/p4lr9yp

the company's bank account, but I didn't feel rich. I felt poor and trapped. I've had less than one-month of rent in my personal account, and I've had enough to cover my expenses for over a year without working. Strangely, I felt the wealthiest when I barely had enough to survive. I can actually remember that moment because I mentioned it to my sister-in-law that day. I was so happy that I felt compelled to tell her.

Don't get me wrong. Having money feels great. I like having it, and I'm sure you do too. But money is a tool, and nothing more. Don't confuse it with the end-goal. Getting rich isn't just about hoarding piles of cash in a vault. Here are some other ways to get rich:

- Gain Knowledge
- Build Relationships
- Have Experiences
- Build Products You Love
- Find Your Maximum Contribution
- Secure Your Future

Let's dig into these a bit further...

Gaining Knowledge

James Altucher talks about the power of the "idea muscle" in his book, *Choose Yourself.* His wife, Claudia Altucher, has written another book about it called

Become an Idea Machine. Flexing the idea muscle is just like flexing any other muscle. It gets stronger with repetition. With enough practice, you'll solve problems more easily, write more effectively, and think more freely. Better productivity, better opportunities, and a better income will then follow.

You can flex your idea muscle by deliberately focusing on it. Read blog posts and books. Listen to podcasts. Keep an idea journal and write down a few ideas a day (James recommends at least ten). Because writing is such a thoughtful activity, it almost forces you to flex your idea muscle and gain knowledge.

Building Relationships

Throughout the process of writing a book, you'll inevitably reach out to awesome people. You'll link up with other authors and thought-leaders. Your book's message will put you in social spheres with like-minded people. Writing a book is arguably the best way to meet incredible people without forcing it. And when you meet incredible people, the richness in your life—and your future opportunities for growth—are bound to expand.

I can remember a sunny spring day a few years after my first book was published. I was at a house party, and I happened to be sitting across from the guy who sold Marvel Studios to Disney and cast Robert Downey Jr.

"Five years from now, you're the same person except for the people you've met and the books you've read." [†]

—JOHN WOODEN

† https://tinyurl.com/yaffqz2h

as Ironman. Everyone else at the party was similarly amazing. Some of the smartest people in the world were there. I never would have thought I'd be in contact with people like that, but it wasn't by chance. I can trace all of it back to the day I decided to write my first book. It set me along a path to meet amazing people.

As we move into the Relationship Economy, the ability to connect with influential people will be a prerequisite for our next wave of leaders. And even if you don't want to be a leader, this still matters. Relationships are a far better solution for surfacing work opportunities, versus having a nice resume or a college degree.

Having Experiences

Writing a book is a grand endeavor. It's hard. But don't think of it as a chore. Think of it as an *experience*. A journey. An adventure.

Working on big ideas makes life worthwhile. Some of my best memories over the past decade involve writing books. I can remember pacing around my room, leaping over to the computer as an idea struck, soaking in a jacuzzi while editing chapters, walking along the beach to clear my mind, and writing late into the night. I can distinctly remember interviewing people, talking to publishers, and working with audio producers and book designers. It was a huge undertaking, full of ups and downs. But it was also incredibly rewarding.

Building Products You Believe In

I've built various products: Games, apps, blogs, books, etc. Writing has given me the most personal satisfaction and wealth, without a doubt. Books are usually a labor of love. It's hard for them not to be. Why else would you take on such a daunting task? (Hint: If it's just for money or fame, you're doing it wrong.) To me, getting rich isn't about having money. It's about feeling free and controlling how I spend my time.

Finding Your Maximum Contribution

When energy is coursing through your veins and you're thinking faster than your fingers can type, you're in the Zone. You're in a state of maximum contribution. When you're in that state, you won't worry about what you're missing on Facebook, or which TV show comes on next, or how much money you could be making doing something else. Instead, you'll get lost in the moment and lose track of everything *except* that moment. And when you put that type of high-octane energy into the world, the world acknowledges it and sends it back.

Getting rich is being happy. Being happy is a result of the pursuits I'm describing. Money is awesome too, but if you do what I say, opportunities involving money will find you. You have to put in the effort. You can't sit on the couch and hope to have amazing experiences. You can't watch TV all day and still have time to write your book. Getting rich takes hard work, and it's a long grind.

It was initially strange to me that I was more stressed when I owned a large portion of a multimillion-dollar company than when I had less than a month of rent in my bank account (which, by the way, happened *after* building the company, not beforehand). I've asked myself how this could be possible, and it comes down to control. There were other people driving the decisions at my first startup. I had become a passenger in my own life. When you aren't the captain of whatever you're working on, you feel strain from others. That strain can quickly morph into stress.

Feeling powerless to say "no" is debilitating. If you want to be rich, you need to disconnect from that environment and find another where you feel free—a place where you can flex your idea muscle and get support instead of resistance. A place where *you* call the shots. When you're in charge of your own destiny, there's still stress, but you have complete control over it. As you journey through life, do you want to be on offense or defense? You'll never score big if you're simply taking orders and reacting.

Securing Your Future

Delving into the entrepreneurial project of writing a book puts you on offense, and it will help you get rich in every area of your life. When you're writing, you're a producer. You're an inventor. You're a *maker*. Will there be obstacles? Haters? Of course. But *you* get to control the narrative. *You* get to decide who to listen to and who to ignore. And then you get to distribute and publish your product, without any pressures but your own. The likelihood of making a million dollars directly from book sales, while possible, is low. But the likelihood of building a *rich* life, in all aspects of the word, is incredibly high.

> **Getting real:** If you thought I'd cop out and *not* talk about the money in a literal, actionable way, you're wrong. I know you care about the money. That's why I'm giving you hard numbers throughout the book.

I launched *The Connection Algorithm* as a first-time author and immediately started earning over a thousand dollars per month. I launched *Hustle* six months later and saw similar results. My passive income was roughly $20,000 in the first year, and I never really optimized my distribution or marketing. I also used my books to build a business that hit six figures in its first year. Because I'm playing the long game with my books, I'm optimizing for rankings and units-sold versus short-term profit. I know the books are part of a bigger strategy to continually promote other related products and services.

Putting this all together, earning a six-figure income from self-publishing books is a reasonable expectation for anyone willing to put in the time and effort. There's also the possibility of getting into the seven or eight-figure range, especially if you use your book(s) to launch related businesses. There are plenty of examples in this book to prove that out. Unlike a corporate job, there's no ceiling.

Books Make You Credible

Who is more impressive? The person who tells you she knows a lot about marketing, or the person who wrote a #1 bestselling book about it? Most people talk the talk, but very few of us walk the walk. A book provides tangible evidence that you know what you're doing. It establishes you as an authority.

You might be thinking, *"Wait, I don't consider myself an authority. Who am I to make that claim?"* Don't worry. That's a natural reaction. I feel that way all the time. The truth is that writing a good book requires critical thinking and learning. Even if you weren't an expert going in, you'll be an expert by the time you're done.

Establishing credibility, specifically through a book, can create a strong funnel (or "welcome mat") to your brand. It can direct people to other products you create. You'll also be more likely to land speaking gigs, become a contributing writer for various publications, appear on podcasts, etc.

Shortly after my first book was released, I booked an appearance on Entrepreneur On Fire, a top ten business podcast that has over one million monthly downloads from listeners in 145 countries around the world. Their acceptance rate for guests is less than 15%. I was able to land the interview because I wrote a bestselling book. Without the book, there's no way I would have made the cut. And of course, I was able to *promote* the book during the interview. See how that works? It's a virtuous cycle that keeps feeding on itself.

Books Help You Grow

The act of writing carries immense personal value. Similar to exercising, you won't feel the benefits unless you practice consistently—but it's worth it. Here are a few of the byproducts:

- A good writer is a good communicator
- A good writer is a good thinker
- A good writer is a good organizer
- A good writer is passionate

- A good writer is a producer
- A good writer is accomplished
- A good writer is an expert

A good writer is a good communicator.
When you write, you must consider how the audience will perceive your message. Because you aren't engaged in a real-time conversation, you can craft your words carefully. This is why people often prefer writing an email over making a phonecall to describe a complex situation.

Writing is usually the best option in these scenarios, but even when the circumstances require speaking in person, the practice of writing will help you perform better off-the-cuff, too. Improving your writing naturally sharpens your communication skills in general. This is valuable in *any* team environment, and the majority of our society is bad at it. Want to stay ahead of the pack? Become a good writer.

A good writer is a good thinker.
To describe something, we must first understand it. Then we must communicate it *effectively*.

I wrote product specification documents for our engineers at my first startup. It was insanely difficult. The documents had to be clear and concise. There was no room for ambiguity. Word choice was very

"If you are trying to decide among a few people to fill a position, hire the best writer."

—JASON FRIED & DAVID HEINEMEIER, *Rework*

important. Removing content was just as important as the clarity of the content that remained. I was really bad at it. I never felt completely competent at spec writing, but I got better over time, and that's the lesson. Just keep writing and you'll improve.

A good writer is a good organizer.
Should your book be long or short? Should you open with a summary of the content to follow, or leave the summary for the end? How does the current paragraph relate to the next? How does it relate to the last? Should you break your thoughts up into smaller sections, or does the material flow better in fewer, larger sections?

When you write, you're organizing your thoughts. It helps you understand how you think and how others think. This organizational skill is incredibly valuable and applicable to any project you might be working on. Structuring a book is just as important as the content itself. This is why content editors exist, but you shouldn't rely on them. If you pay attention to structure from the beginning, you'll write a better book.

A good writer is passionate.
When we're caught up in the hustle and bustle of the day, it's easy to lose track of our interests. We quickly become preoccupied with the task at hand, or the never-erending to-do list looming in the back of our minds.

Writing, by contrast, will naturally reveal your passions and beliefs. It's enlightening.

Take time to sit down and write about something you care about. It will force you to discard the distractions of the day. Thinking critically only happens through focus, and writing forces this focus. You may not realize your passion until you start experiencing it through writing. It sounds strange, but give it a try. When I was working at my first startup, I found myself writing late into night, and again in the mornings. I couldn't escape it. Those bursts of mindless writing became the genesis of *The Connection Algorithm*, which became a bestseller. I never could have planned for that. It was born out of pure passion.

A good writer is a Producer.
There are two categories of people in this world—Producers and Consumers.[7] As the names suggest, Consumers *consume* content, while Producers *produce* content. When you write, you put yourself in the Producer category, which is empowering.

Sharing your knowledge, your thoughts, and your creativity with the world creates value. Do you want to be the person on the stage or the person in the audience? If you want to on stage, you need to be a

---

7 Yes, of course you can seesaw between both.

Producer. Later, we'll discuss the next evolution of our society, which I call *The Creation Age*. In The Creation Age, Producers hold all the power.

A good writer is accomplished.

In today's digital world, writing is one of the most effective ways to build your brand. When you write publicly, you're demonstrating your ambition and your initiative as a Producer. You're sharing your knowledge. You're sharing your passion. You're sharing *yourself*. The internet has given us a platform to bring value to billions of people with the click of a button, so writing publicly allows you to contribute to the world while simultaneously strengthening your own individual stock.

A good writer is an expert.

Ultimately, if you practice the craft of writing, you will become an expert in whatever you're writing about. This is different from credibility, which is the *perception* of expertise. I'm talking about actual knowledge. Do you think it's a coincidence that some of the most influential and successful business people are also prolific writers? Tim Ferriss, Brad Feld, Fred Wilson, Ben Horowitz, Eric Ries, Reid Hoffman, and Peter Thiel are a few names that come to mind.

The assumption is that these people write because

they're experts, but what if it's the other way around? What if they're experts because they write? When I look at these people, I notice another common thread: *Their success has longevity*. How does one stay abreast of the most critical influences within our constantly changing environment? How does one continuously refine his craft and stay sharp? How does one affect others in his field, such that he stays relevant and valuable? I think you know the answer.

Books Make You Immortal

There's a much bigger reason to write a book than anything I've mentioned thus far—perhaps the ultimate reason: *It makes you immortal*. It stamps your legacy into the halls of eternity.

Randy Pausch was a professor of computer science at Carnegie Mellon, but he won't be remembered for that. He'll be remembered for the book he co-authored, *The Last Lecture*.[8] He wrote it for his nine-month old daughter as he was dying from pancreatic cancer.

Randy's death is heartbreaking, but there's a bittersweet ending. Even though his daughter never met him in the traditional sense, she knows him well. His prose, which she was able to read years later, taught her more than most parents can claim of their

---

8 https://tinyurl.com/yaxzkajq

children. And that's not all. Randy has since touched the hearts of *millions*. His book became a bestseller. It was translated into forty-eight languages and has sold over five million copies in the US alone. Randy died of cancer, but he'll live on forever inside the pages of *The Last Lecture*.

If your life was taken from you today, what would you leave behind? Some Facebook status updates? Some photos? Some tweets? What if your children and grandchildren never got to meet you? What would they know of you? Without a book, your thoughts are nothing more than spilled blood. They're lost forever. But if you write them down, they live on. Your children, and *their* children, will know you. People beyond your family might get to know you, too. Maybe hundreds of people. Maybe thousands. Maybe even *millions*.

Writing makes you immortal. It gives you the power to change lives—to engage with the world for all eternity. The influence of one mind is immeasurable, and nearly all of us can now share our wisdom at near zero cost, without anyone's permission. Will you harness that power, or let it die with your heartbeat? The choice is yours.

CHAPTER 3

BECOMING AN AUTHORPRENEUR

Before confronting the blinking cursor on your screen, let's consider whether or not you have what it takes to write a book with an entrepreneurial approach. To succeed, you'll need three specific skills, plus a high level of commitment. I'll discuss these skills in this section.[1] I'll also explain what every author is selling,

---

1 Take note that these skills transcend professions. The recipe for becoming a successful writer is also the recipe for becoming successful in general.

and more importantly, *how* to sell effectively. Finally, I'll debunk the most common book-publishing myths so you can stop worrying and start writing.

Three Critical Traits to Succeed as a Writer

You need three critical traits to successfully write and launch your book. They are: Work ethic, vision, and problem-solving. Let's define those a bit further.

Work Ethic: Energy, inspiration, and hustle. The ability to grind, withstand downturns, and confront uncertainty.

Vision: Seeing the goal before it materializes. More specifically, an innate sense of *quality*. You need to produce a high-quality product, which means attention to detail, an understanding of your market, and an accurate pulse on consumer expectations. A visionary understands the importance of both effort *and* execution. A common misstep is building the wrong product—meaning people either never wanted it, or it isn't good enough. The quality bar is impossible to measure. It must be felt.

Problem-Solving: The ability to solve any problem and learn whatever is necessary to achieve the desired outcome. Everyone has great ideas, but most people give up when things get tough. Very few people can execute to completion. Here's one of my favorite quotes:

"Vision is not enough; it must be combined with venture. It is not enough to stare up the steps; we must step up the stairs." —Vaclav Havel.

You can't succeed unless you possess all three traits, or assemble a team to fill the gaps. You can have work ethic and problem-solving skills, but if you produce a low quality product, it won't sell. You can have work ethic and vision, but if you don't have problem-solving skills, you'll hit a wall and won't know how to break through it. And similarly, if you have the ability to solve problems and an eye for quality, but don't have work ethic, you'll lose motivation and never finish.

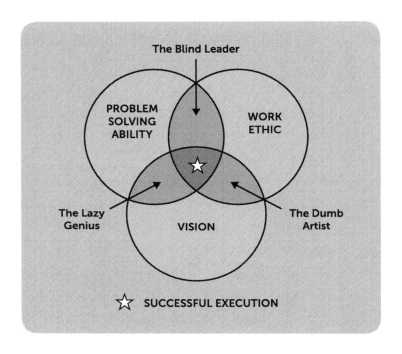

Now for some brutal honesty: Most of the people who read this book won't follow through. They'll feel inspired, but fail to take action. Or they'll get started, and then give up after hitting a speed bump. Or they'll complete the project, but in a half-hearted way that doesn't provide value. Are you the rare breed who can put in the effort, sustain it, and produce great work? I have faith that you are![2]

---

2 *Note:* If you're weak in one or more areas, you can certainly still succeed. You just need to build a team that collectively covers the bases. Some of the best entrepreneurs are team-builders.

Resist the Hack. Embrace the Grind.

In 2010, Rich Roll completed the Epic5 Challenge, a series of five ironman-distance triathlons on five Hawaiian islands, in less than seven days. Ironman triathlons consist of a 2.4-mile swim, a 112-mile bicycle ride, and a 26.2-mile marathon run, raced in that order, and without a break.[3] Rich did *five of those in seven days.* By the way, he only eats plants.

If you ask Rich how he did this, he'll likely tell you it's all in the grind. Rich doesn't prepare for triathlons. Instead, he lives in a constant state of training. Rich loves the grind, or as many people call it, the journey. He wrote about this in a memoir titled, *Finding Ultra: Rejecting Middle Age, Becoming One of the World's Fittest Men, and Discovering Myself.* It became a #1 bestseller, and still topped the Amazon charts years after its initial publication date.

One of the biggest takeaways from Rich's story is his undying dedication to not only achieving greatness, but *maintaining* it. He doesn't believe in finish lines. Instead, he embraces the daily grind of doing meaningful, purposeful work. In a culture increasingly focused on tips, tricks, hacks, and shortcuts (all of which I'm admittedly guilty of preaching about on some level), Rich's deliberate confrontation and

_____

3 https://tinyurl.com/ps2kyky

appreciation of *the grind* is refreshing. He wrote an amazing blog post about this.[4] Here are a few excerpts, because I can't say it any better:

> *"Consistent with our shrinking attention span, demand for immediate gratification, intolerance for hard work, rebuttal of experiential value, and general (illusory) sense of entitlement to the good life, this hack ethos is emblematic of our obsessive modern imperative for immediacy — the drive to turbocharge, accelerate, optimize, scramble, quicken and hasten our way to maximum health, fitness, professional success and ultimately happiness. A hell-bent zeal to quick-fix ourselves to overnight six-pack abs, envious wealth, limitless free time, and in some ways I suppose, salvation. Finger-snap your way to nirvana. Don't just keep up with The Joneses — blow them out of the water!*
>
> *...It used to be an insult to call someone a hack. Now it's high praise. How did a term so historically pejorative suddenly become aspirational?"*

---

4 https://tinyurl.com/ydcrwcgn

Rich believes our life-hacking mindset is being driven largely by popular media, especially breakout hits like *The Four Hour Workweek,* by Tim Ferriss. He doesn't take issue with what Tim teaches. (In fact, he and Tim are close friends.) He just feels the overall message has become skewed over time.

"In truth, a properly implemented hack is nothing more than leveraging a good idea (I guess #idea or #goodidea don't really trend well when it comes to the meme-o-sphere). A way to cut wasted time so that you can invest yourself more fully in what makes your heart truly beat—a passion and pursuit that can transform your life by catalyzing a new journey.

I take no issue with this. It's great, actually. And I think this is what Tim was actually trying to say.

But somewhere along the line I think even Tim would agree that we lost the thread. Somewhere along the line, the hack has become the destination, rather than the tool. An end in and of itself. Kind of like becoming obsessed with a table saw rather than the process of using it to learn how to make a beautiful piece of furniture.

Moreover, the explosion of hack culture seems to inherently disrespect the paramount value of the journey—the true value in any experience—by supplanting it with an expedited rush to access to a result. And result is empty without grappling with the resistance that inevitably defines the battle."

The true value of any pursuit lies in *the process of reaching for something great*—not necessarily the moment of grasping it.

"Now let's examine what happens when you try to be the very best you can be at something you are inherently passionate about. Suddenly the heart beats faster. The palms begin to sweat. Maybe it's excitement. But more likely it's fear. That's right, fear. Commitment—total dedication to the core—is about as scary as it gets. It's not just hard. It's without a doubt the most difficult thing imaginable. Because if you take that risk, truly put yourself completely on the line and fail (or succeed—yes fear of success plagues more than you might imagine), then you will have to reckon with yourself. Terrifying!

But that is the whole point and purpose. Failure

(or success) — or at least the prospect of failure (or success) — is what gives the journey proper context, rich consistency, and towering emotional, physical, financial and spiritual stakes that fertilize the soul for quantum growth irrespective of outcome. And growth is everything. But it can only result from earnest investment in experience. So fear and commitment aren't things to be avoided, but rather embraced with a bear hug of everything."

There are a few lessons here:

1. Let go of the "quick-win" strategy. As Rich says, hacking is great for the day-to-day. But to do truly meaningful work, you need to embrace the grind.

2. Work on things you're innately passionate about. This fuels your energy as you push through your fear. This very moment, I'm writing the sentence you'll hopefully be reading in the future. The words are flowing onto the page, and they'll eventually come together to form a book. Is there fear it might not work out? That it might not sell? That it might flop? Yes. There's intense fear. But that's when I know I'm onto something

meaningful. The fire in my fingertips keeps me going. The work I'm doing right now is passionate work. And that's enough.

3. If you embrace the grind, you'll have a richer life, and therefore better material for your book. What's more exciting: 1. The story of the guy who sits on the couch, or 2. the story of the guy who launches ten companies, fails miserably at all of them, becomes a surfer, and finally finds passion by raising his children on the waves? The second story, although littered with "failure," is far more compelling. So failure, as we typically define it, is never really a bad thing. It's actually an ingredient for interesting stories about risk and growth, which adds color to the otherwise uneventful timeline of life. The man on the couch has no stories to tell. No risk, no failure, and no success. No nothing.

4. If you want to write a good book, go on some ill-advised adventures, or find people who do, and write about *them*. Most importantly, don't look for the hack. Embrace the grind.

No One Cares What You Do

Gut check. Have you ever gone to a cocktail party, and someone asks, "What do you do?" It's my least favorite question.

You start explaining. Heads start nodding, eyes start glazing over, and it quickly becomes apparent that nobody really cares. It's okay. It's not your fault. Almost universally, we don't care about what other people are doing. Or maybe it's not that we don't care—but that it's just hard to understand what anyone actually does beyond a surface level.

There are billions of people on this planet, and we're all naturally focused on our own lives. This means you can't rely on others for validation or encouragement while writing your book. When you tell people about it, you probably won't get more than a half-hearted nod, at best (unless you're telling your mother). So you need to believe in what you're doing. *You,* at the core, have to believe it's valuable.

It might seem like you're the only one who cares, but you're not. There are plenty of others. They're just not sitting directly in front of you. If you follow the guidelines I've laid out in Part Two, they'll eventually find your book through a keyword search, or a podcast, or a blog post. The internet will reveal your fans. As you write, think of yourself—and your eventual fans. That's it.[5]

---

5 You should still validate your market. More on that in Part Two.

Greg: Do you remember ABC?

Seth: Yeah, Always Be Closing.

—THE BOILER ROOM

You're a Salesman

I don't like pushing products on people. When I was a boy, the doorbell would ring in the middle of the day. Most of the time it was a salesman. He would say, "hello," and then awkwardly jump into a sales pitch. He would try to sell us a new water filtration system, or a better vacuum cleaner, or a better religion. It was annoying.

What aggravated me wasn't the selling—it was the *approach* to selling, and the stuff being sold. I don't need a better vacuum cleaner. I'm a minimalist. I don't like having a lot of stuff. But I care deeply about health and knowledge. If someone I trust wants to sell me a life-changing supplemental drink, I'll listen. If a friend recommends a book, I'll check it out.

Do you see what I'm saying? We're all salespeople. When we go on a date, we're selling our personality. When we defend our opinions, we're selling our beliefs. When we apply for a job, we're selling our skills. When we write a blog post, we're selling our ideas. The distinction between a good salesman and a bad one is the motivation behind the selling, and the effort in selling to the right people.

Accept that you're a salesman, but let *passion* be your product, and let *pride* be your payment. Think about how the transaction helps *the other person*, not how it helps you. Frame it as sharing your worth. If you're contributing value to the other person, it feels good to sell that value.

Have faith that you're worth it, but try to find people who actually *want* your product. I don't tell everyone about my books. I only tell people who might find them useful. If they don't seem interested, I move on. I'm not here to convert *everyone* into writers and entrepreneurs. I'm here to find people who legitimately want to take that leap, but haven't yet found the courage.

The happiest, most successful people are passionate salesmen. They're CEOs selling a vision, freelancers selling talent, bloggers selling ideas, teachers selling knowledge, and parents selling love.

You should quietly sell your value by contributing to the world with purpose, explaining what drives you, and sharing your very best work. This type of selling doesn't feel like selling. It feels like giving.

Book Myths

There are a bunch of myths around writing books. We tend to overcomplicate the whole process, create unnecessary roadblocks, and trick ourselves into thinking tasks are harder than they are. This happens because *we're scared*. We use these myths as an excuse to avoid getting started. Well, I'm about to tear them down so you'll be free and clear to move forward.

Myth #1: You need to be an expert.

I touched on this earlier, but let's confront it head-on. What makes someone an expert? A college degree? Years of practice? Awards and accolades? There's no right answer. I've read fabulous books by professors and PhDs, but I've also read fabulous books by college dropouts. Instead of worrying about the common formulas for measuring intelligence and qualification, simply ask yourself if you can provide value.

Am I an "expert" in writing and publishing books? I don't know. I've done book launches for various clients. I've published two of my own. The books I've published have done relatively well, and I've learned a lot about the industry in general. Is that enough? Spoiler alert: It doesn't matter. I know I can provide valuable information and help people.

Leo Babauta runs a blog called Zen Habits. His articles teach people how to form habits and live a fulfilling life. The blog reaches over a million readers per month. Is Leo an expert? What are his credentials? He addresses this question on his blog:

> *"So you're reading some of my posts on how to achieve your goals, and how to save money or exercise or wake up early, and you're wondering, what exactly are my qualifications? My answer is that I have no formal qualifications. I am not*

an expert, or a doctor, or a coach.

I haven't made millions of dollars and I'm not the world's greatest athlete. All I am is a regular guy, a father of six kids, a husband, a writer from Guam (now living in San Francisco). But I have accomplished a lot over the last couple of years (and failed a lot) and along the way, I have learned a lot."[6]

Being an expert is arbitrary and subjective. To create value, you must simply connect with your readers. Leo says insightful things, so his readers listen.

Myth #2: You should heavily research your market to see if there's a need.
Wrong. I didn't do much market research for this book. That might sound crazy, but the reasons are simple.

1. Value sells.
2. Knowledge is always valuable.
3. Books (specifically digital books) are an emerging product category.
4. You'll never attain 100% clarity.

---

6 http://zenhabits.net/my-story/

I don't need to figure out if people are interested in learning how to successfully write a book or become an entrepeneur. There are over a million books available on Kindle. Why spend time researching or trying to quantify the opportunity? *It's very big.* That's all I need to know.

There's no way to accurately measure the true size of the need, or the particular segment I might be able to capture. I don't need to do a survey or create a focus group. That's just wasted energy that will give me more *excuses* to not move forward. I instead need to take the leap and trust people will find value in what I have to say. I wouldn't have much more certainty of the outcome after researching, so it's a pointless exercise.

Note that *competitive research* is different from *learning*. I constantly read books that relate to the topics I write about. This happens naturally because I'm genuinely interested in whatever I'm reading. While I'm reading, I'm learning. So when I decide to write a book, I already know there's a market for that type of book, and have a good pulse on the existing literature. It's also good to do a quick market research hacking exercise (described in Part Two), but that only takes a few hours at most.

Myth #3: You need to constantly analyze and review your competition.

Wrong. I didn't do any competitive analysis for this book. There are undoubtedly related books out there, but that doesn't bother me. It simply validates my concept. I know I have valuable things to say—content that will make people think, plus practical, actionable guidance. Value is the only element required for long-term sales, so don't focus on your competition. Focus on the value you're sharing.

If you feel the need to constantly check up on your competition, you don't know enough about the topic you're writing about. Looking at similar content too much also makes you a "me too" product. It puts you behind the curve. You want to be riding the wave, not paddling along behind it.

Again, you should already have a base of knowledge. It's perfectly fine to refer back to similar books. I do that all the time. Pull relevant quotes and use existing content to build your argument. But don't mimic another book entirely. You should be bringing something new to the table and using your own unique voice.

Myth #4: The product needs to deliver unparalleled value to be successful and sell.

Wrong. The cost of a digital book is such that it doesn't need to deliver mind-blowing value to sell. Obviously I want to provide as much value as possible—and I hope this book is life-changing for you. But if it's not, you're not going to beat yourself up about it, or hunt me down and poke me with a pitchfork.

Amazon has done a great service to authors. They've created a platform that psychologically conditions consumers to pay. People expect to pay at least $0.99 for a Kindle book. The platform also makes it possible to price books lower than ever before, since almost all manufacturing costs disappear when the final product is a digital file. This is a win for both consumers *and* authors.

In the past, a consumer might be upset if they spent $30 on a book and it was only mildly useful. But today, the same book can be offered for only a few dollars. The result is a more forgiving audience, and a more flexible market for books that range in length, content, and style.

Don't misunderstand—you should always aim for quality content. The best quality still rises to the top. But the Long Tail is getting fatter, which is good for everyone.

Myth #5: Repetition is to be avoided. People want fresh content.

Wrong again. While you shouldn't mimic an existing book page-by-page, people love recurring concepts. It builds validation and usually reveals slightly varying perspectives that can then be triangulated by the reader. I deliberately use repetition throughout this book. I even incorporate ideas that were introduced in my previous books. Repetition is reinforcement. And people are forgetful, remember?

The Creation Age

Welcome to the era of the Producer. Because making stuff is so much easier today than it was twenty years ago (and because society takes a while to catch up), being a Producer is a powerful differentiator. Soon, it will be a commodity. People won't ask, "Where did you go to school?" Instead, they'll ask, "What have you created? What product have you actually built?"

Our world now runs on platforms, most of which require little or no capital to use. If you haven't built something, what are you doing with your time? Most likely, you're just consuming.

Thought leaders like Naval Ravikant believe we're entering the Entrepreneur Economy, an economy governed by the *self.* A recent exodus from the traditional workplace and subsequent surges in freelancing and startups have already confirmed this trend.[7] As the world's power shifts to the individual, those who can *create* will be in the highest demand, which is why I call it *The Creation Age.*

While it might sound scary, it's actually a good thing. This is an unbelievably empowering time to be alive. You're standing in the eye of the storm—a beautiful and powerful storm. You live in a reality where everyone can be an inventor. Think of all the Franklins and Platos and Aristotles and Freuds and Einsteins that will inevitably emerge from this perfect mixture of technology, communication, and freedom. Maybe *you,* with this book in your hands, will create something revolutionary—something that changes the world forever. The stars have aligned for you to take that leap and make it happen. It's time to jump.

---

7 There are numerous single-employee companies already leveraging the tools afforded by the Creation Age and earning seven-figure incomes. Here's an article with a few good examples: https://tinyurl.com/q4b97hk

CRAFTING AND LAUNCHING YOUR BESTSELLER

Congratulations! You've finished the philosophical portion of this book. You should now understand why this is the best time in history to write and launch a book of your own. Part Two explores how to make it happen. I've organized Part Two into categories, charting out all the tasks you should complete as you march toward launching your book. At the end of each chapter, you'll find a summary that includes links to the Authorpreneur Companion Course. All the resources referenced in the chapter are accessible from the course website.

Because self-publishing is the best option for most authors (especially first-timers), we'll be focusing on a self-publishing approach, so let's first define that term.

What is Self-Publishing?

A self-published book is any publicly available work still owned by the original author. Many of the up-and-coming publishers are allowing authors to keep the rights to their work (or a majority of it). I consider that a self-published book. Self-publishing doesn't mean you're publishing by yourself. It just means you're the primary owner of your work. If you want to be successful, you'll need to work with various third parties to create a professional product worthy of a mainstream audience, whether you use a traditional publisher or not.

I'm not against traditional publishers. I'm against the current process of working with the entrenched players, especially as a new author. I recommend self-publishing initially. If you have success with your self-published title and a traditional publisher approaches you with an amazing offer you can't refuse, don't blindly decline it. It could be worth it once you have some early traction and leverage.

The Overnight Success

Have you ever heard the terms "overnight success," or "get rich quick"? They're buzzwords. *They don't actually exist.*

Creating anything of value takes time and effort. Writing a book is no exception. It's a big undertaking. Even though I wrote and published *Hustle* in seven days, I had already spent months building up a brand and learning how to market it and launch it.

After publishing a book, the work doesn't stop. I say this not to discourage you, but to manage your expectations. There's considerable work that contributes to a successful launch and sustained sales. In the following chapters, I'll take you through the steps. Keep in mind, you can write and publish a book on very short timelines, as I did for my book, *Hustle*. But what follows is the approach I recommend for most people.

CHAPTER 4

BUILD YOUR BRAND

The 50% Rule: Or, Stop Writing and Start Selling

When I wrote my first book, I didn't understand the importance of branding and marketing. Simply put, marketing should be half of your effort, or more.

I learned this the hard way. I thought if I wrote compelling content, I'd be able to find an agent or a publisher who would promote my book. Unfortunately, that's not how the industry works.

Publishers and agents want to see that you already have an established following. Otherwise, they won't

"This is what we call the 50% rule: Spend 50% of your time on product and 50% on traction."

—GABRIEL WEINBERG, *Traction*

work with you. Here's the good news: *you don't need to worry about getting a publisher.* If you subscribe to my approach, it's not the best initial route to take anyway.

Still, I spent countless hours exploring traditional publishing to get a ground-level perspective on it. Here's a quick rundown of that model (compiled not only from research, but from friends who've partnered with traditional publishers in the past):

1. Publishers won't help you market your book. They want you to have your own following.

2. Most publishers will take a huge chunk of your profits, sometimes up to 95%, often leaving you with almost nothing.

3. If you're not already a bestselling author, you'll get a *very* small advance—a few thousand bucks, if you're lucky.

4. It can take *years* for your book to actually get released. Publishers often have a backlist of other titles to produce, and your book could get bumped, paused, or shelved if more compelling projects emerge in the meantime. The publisher's goal is to maximize their overall profit, not necessarily *your* profit.

5. The biggest benefits a publisher can provide include: editing, book design, logistics, a fancy-looking crest on your book's spine, and distribution in bookstores. But guess what? All of those things either don't matter anymore, or can now be done on your own—*cheaply* and *easily*. I'll show you how.

Here are some quotes from email exchanges I've had with published authors and industry insiders:

> "A publisher would want to see a bigger marketing platform and following. Of course this is assuming you want a traditional publisher. For example, if you had a very popular website or Facebook following because you had good advice or interesting interviews with some of the luminaries you know, you might be able to parlay that following into a book contract. Publishers like sure things, like, 'Oh, his online fans already know him and will buy his book.' I'm not saying that is easy to do, but that is what they're looking for."
>
> —A very respected agent

> "Traditional publishers are not great, and they are slow. Advances are tiny (if you even get one)

*and publishers may even make you agree to buy
a certain number of your own books!"*

—A friend who published
with McGraw Hill

"It should be easier for more people to write and produce high quality, useful, long-form books. While we think the entire process and engagement model is completely broken, that leads us to the punchline of the thing that is really wrong.

The relationship between the reader and the author has an immense amount of friction in it. And that friction comes from the publisher. It's not just that the economics are wrong (why should the economic split between publisher and author be — on average — 85% to the publisher and 15% to the author?) but that the publisher sits in between the author and the reader."

*—My friend and accomplished
author Brad Feld*

So if you're a first-time author (or even an established one), traditional publishing probably isn't your optimal route. I just saved you a bunch of headaches. You're welcome. The bad news: *You still need a following.*

No matter how you slice it, you need to create a platform to drive people to your content. It's not going to sell itself. So, what should you do to build your online presence? Read on to find out.

Create a Personal Site

Launching a blog or website is a good way to establish your digital home base. I didn't blog before writing my first book because I convinced myself it would fail and I'd look like an idiot. Don't do this! It's not a smart way to go into a launch. Besides, the logic is faulty. If your book doesn't sell, no one will know about it anyway. Do you know the names of the movies starring Tom Cruise that flopped? No. You only know the hits.

Bottom line—if you don't have a blog or site, you're giving yourself a higher mountain to climb. When you blog, you establish yourself as an influencer in your field. A blog can also prompt new content for the book itself. And perhaps most importantly, you can use your blog to build an email list. More on that later.

For the most flexible website possible, I recommend using Wordpress. Why? Because all the services for collecting emails and editing the design are compatible with Wordpress. Many of them are not compatible with other services like SquareSpace, Wix, or Weebly. Trust me on this. This single piece of advice alone will save you hundreds of dollars down the road. You'll also need a hosting service to host your site. I recommend Bluehost. Michael Hyatt has a great post on setting up your site. Just Google: "launch a self-hosted wordpress blog Michael Hyatt," and it will pop right up.

Create Landing Pages

A landing page is a webpage with a single focus. Usually, that focus is to either sell something, or collect an email, which is called a "'lead." Once you have someone's email, you can communicate with them and eventually sell them something. In this case, we're selling books. There are companies that allow you to create landing pages without knowing how to code. My favorite is LeadPages. Other options include Unbounce and Instapage. With LeadPages, you can connect your landing pages to your website-or use it as a stand alone solution.

You should create a landing page for your book even before it's written. On the landing page, explain what the book is about. You can use the page to collect email and offer your book for free to anyone who signs up. This is called a "lead magnet." By giving the person a gift, they'll be more likely to give you their email. I'll explain why you should do this later, but the main idea is that you can use your book to create a group of early adopters. Those people can be valuable in the future, even though they're not paying you any money for the book up front.

Using this method, I collected nearly 1,000 emails from early adopters who wanted to read this book before it was written. (To see the landing page I created, check out the free resources at the end of the chapter.)

If technology scares you, you might prefer a tool called Welcome Mat, which is offered by the company, Sumo.com. You can use Welcome Mat to create a landing page with only a few clicks. The feature adds a call-to-action directly to your homepage, asking visitors to join your email list. It takes up the entire screen initially, but users can simply scroll down to see the rest of your site. Here's an example of Welcome Mat (All content and styling is customizable):

This works extremely well because it focuses the reader's attention. The average reader will only spend 15 seconds on your site, so you want to capture their email as quickly as possible. Simplifying the page by presenting a single call-to-action significantly increases your chances of achieving the intended result (an email submission) within those precious moments.

Creating content on your own website probably won't bring you significant traffic unless you already have a well-known personal brand. To get more people to your website and landing pages, you should publish content elsewhere.

Publish Content on Other Platforms

While you're in the process of writing your book, you should craft related articles and publish them on other content platforms like Medium, Influencive, or ThoughtCatalog. You can even publish content directly from your book as you write.

Throughout each article, find logical places in the content to direct people back to your landing pages or website. You should also include a link at the end of each article. Here's an example:

This is effective because platforms like Medium and ThoughtCatalog have massive audiences.

Instead of writing a post on your own site and getting only five people to look at it, you'll be tapping into a pre-existing community. It gives you a much better chance of picking up new readers, who will then be more likely to find their way onto your email list after learning about your free book offering.

Guest Post

Guest posting can also drive traffic to your website and landing pages. It's effective because it gives you access to a new audience and ties you to the brand publishing your content, which adds instant credibility to your work. When I published an article through Sumo.com's website, for example, it received hundreds of shares, generating nearly a hundred new subscribers to my email list within a few months. That was for a single article. You can see how this strategy can effectively build your list over time.

> **PRO TIP**
> Don't spend all your time guest-posting. It can be a time-suck. Later, we'll discuss podcasting, which is another effective and less time-consuming technique.

Writing is only one way to build your list. You can also use various promotional services to build buzz and awareness.

Using Promo Services

Crowd-Based Platforms

You can use crowdfunding platforms like Kickstarter or Publishizer to raise funds for your project. But more importantly, this is another way to build your email list. I ran a Kickstarter campaign for my first book, which raised nearly $17,000. But that wasn't the most valuable part of it. The most valuable asset was the list of over 100 super fans I collected during the campaign.

Create a Facebook Group

A private Facebook group is one of the best ways to find your biggest fans. Invite people to your group and post material related to the topic of your book. The most active people in the group are your super fans. These people can be leveraged later through various tasks, or filtered into a more high-touch tool, like LaunchTeam.

Set up a Launch Team

Finding a small group of people who truly care about your work can be powerful. These people can take your launch from good to great. They can contribute by sharing on social media during your launch, participating in your crowdfunding campaign, writing early reviews for your book, and providing early feedback on your rough drafts.

Bestselling authors, including Michael Hyatt, Lewis Howes, and Pat Flynn (among others), have used this strategy by creating Facebook groups and organizing their teams within that system. My company,

LaunchTeam, offers products and services based on these techniques as well. You can learn more at www.mylaunchteam.com.

Develop a Marketing Strategy

Planning your overall marketing strategy can be daunting. You can certainly do it yourself, but it's helpful to learn from (or work with) the experts. Some of the biggest players in this space include:

- Tom Morkes
- Jeff Goins
- Tim Grahl
- Chandler Bolt
- Ryan Holiday
- Michael Hyatt

Do yourself a favor by learning about these guys and joining their email lists. They all provide incredibly useful information, whether you end up using their services or not.

TL;DR, Resources, and Next Steps

TL;DR (Summary)

- One year out, you should be focusing on building your brand. Marketing should be 50% of your effort or more.

- Launching a website and writing publicly is the most effective way to get started.

- You should create landing pages to collect emails from people who are interested in the topic of your book. Offer to give them your book for free to entice them to provide their email.

- Writing on your website won't bring you much traffic. Instead, write elsewhere. You can write on blogging platforms, like Medium, or request to guest post on popular sites.

- Beyond writing, you can cultivate a group of early-adopters using LaunchTeam. Then you can leverage those people with other promotional services like KickStarter, Publishizer, etc.

- If you want to create a winning marketing strategy, learn from the experts. Some of the biggest names in the industry include: Tom Morkes, Jeff Goins, Tim Grahl, Chandler Bolt, Ryan Holiday, and Michael Hyatt.

Resources

The full set of resources for this chapter can be found in the Authorpreneur Companion Course. To get the free course and materials, go here:

www.jtev.me/authorpreneur-free-course

Next Steps

Building your brand is a process that's constantly happening in the background. But eventually, you need to start writing your book. In the next section, I'll show you how to pick a topic, how to price your book, and how to structure your writing process so you don't get overwhelmed.

JOEL GERSCHMAN AND HOWARD FINGER

Throughout Part Two of this book, I've sprinkled in some short success stories from past clients, called "Inspiration Breaks." I hope these stories fuel your confidence and help you realize: "If they can do it, I can do it, too." Here's the first story...

Howard Finger was a successful businessman, but he didn't feel like one. He wasn't entirely sure if his business was moving in the right direction and he felt overly stressed in almost every aspect of his life. Then he met Joel Gerschman, a business coach. With the help of their friend Aryeh Goldman, the three began to break apart every area of Howard's business and *life*, reassembling them piece by piece. The focus was on growing the business, but there was an important catch: Every change had to *also* help Howard stay sane, focused, and fulfilled.

The unique approach worked like a charm. Howard was able to achieve new levels of success in his business. But more importantly, he was able to enjoy his life in the process. Joel and Howard decided to enlist LaunchTeam to help them release a book about this story, called *The Mindful Entrepreneur*. The book was published through an Australian publishing house, but LaunchTeam handled the bulk of the marketing efforts, eventually taking *The Mindful Entrepreneur* to #1 bestseller status in multiple categories on Amazon. Joel and Howard have sold thousands of copies to date, and continue to use *The Mindful Entrepreneur* to grow their presence in the market, generate sales, and build their platform.

Here's what Joel had to say: "I can say with confidence that Jesse and Simon are book launch gurus. They helped our book, *The Mindful Entrepreneur*, hit #1 on Amazon across multiple categories and we're still there—six months later, having sold in excess of 5,000 digital and hard copy books in the process! Oh, and they're great guys, too."

Want to launch your own book? You can join the free Authorpreneur Companion Course to download our launch materials and learn more about our process.

www.jtev.me/authorpreneur-free-course

CHAPTER 5

PLAN & WRITE

Why Choosing Your #1 Goal is The First Step

If you don't specify your primary goal in writing your book, you'll quickly lose sight of why you're doing it in the first place. Without that direction, you'll end up traveling down a bunch of rabbit holes, wasting time and money—and potentially sabotaging yourself. Need some ideas? Typical goals include:

- I want to grow my email list
- I want to build authority
- I want to make money

Now, which goal are you tackling? Ranking them by importance will guide your actions. You'll often find that one goal opposes the other, which is why it's so critical to identify a primary focus.

For example, if making money is your top priority, you should choose a niche topic and sell your book for a higher price. This means fewer units sold, but more income per sale. That's great for profit, but not great for growing your email list. If your main goal is list-building, you should write about a broader topic and sell your book at a lower price point (or even give it away for free, as I've suggested).

Pricing Strategies: High Price Niche vs. Low Price Broad

There are two pricing models, with corresponding launch strategies:

1. High Price, Niche
2. Low Price, Broad

High Price, Niche

If your primary goal is making money, consider writing about a very niche topic, providing a ton of value, and pricing your book extremely high. If you choose this model, you'll want to set up your own sales page and use a payment provider like SamCart or ThriveCart. You can increase your price point even further by offering add-on services like courses, consulting, videos, etc. Two examples of this are Authority, by Nathan Barry, and Design+Code, by Meng To.

Low Price, Broad
(Recommended for list-building and your first book)
For this method, you'll launch on Amazon with a lower price point ($0.99-3.99). This option will give you more exposure and, therefore, more opportunity to build your list. Amazon has millions of customers. Every day, those customers are searching for products. By publishing on Amazon, you're gaining access to a massive new audience. Plus, Amazon takes care of production and fulfillment.

The Three Approaches to Finding a Topic

When it comes to finding a topic to write about, you might think the answer is market research. And you'd be half-correct. Market research is good for identifying customer needs (which we'll discuss in the next section), but there's another preliminary step.

Before researching whatever you think is "hot right now," brainstorm topics based on your personal passions and experience. Make sure you're writing about something you truly care about.

Writing for the sake of building a list will likely end badly. The best case scenario is that you'll slog through it and grow your audience, but the worst case? Your audience will see right through you and your book will flop. Here are the three main frameworks I use when brainstorming new topics:

1. **Explain how to do something.**
   Example: *Venture Deals*, by Brad Feld. This book teaches entrepreneurs how to understand and negotiate term sheets.

2. **Offer a strong opinion relating to a trend.**
   Example: *David and Goliath*, by Malcolm Gladwell. This book argues that underdogs often have the advantage.

3. **Tell an interesting story.**
   Example: *Finding Ultra*, by Rich Roll. This book tells the story of Rich Roll's transformation from a sluggish, out-of-shape lawyer into one of the fittest men on the planet.

If you can identify a passion and then combine the three frameworks above to write about it, you'll have a home run. Yes, these are broad suggestions, but they'll get your mind moving in the right direction.

How To Narrow Your Focus

After landing on a topic, you might think it's a good idea to cover that subject as broadly as possible. But you need to get more specific. People read nonfiction books to learn. They don't want to hear the same old story, or some broad, generic solution. So your book should provide specific solutions to specific problems.

You also need to hash out why this is an important issue to solve, and who you're solving it for. Without this directed approach, your book won't find an audience, which means no subscribers to your email list. If you're speaking to everyone, you're speaking to no one. I use a simple exercise to determine the core purpose of my books and narrow the focus. I call it the 3 W's

1. WHO: Who is the audience? (It should be a specific person.)

2. WHAT: What does the book teach the reader?

3. WHY: Why is the book useful and relevant? (Why does it need to be written?)

The actual worksheet I use for this exercise can be found in the free companion course here:

www.jtev.me/authorpreneur-free-course

The Three "P" Technique: Market Research Hacks

Once you've decided on a topic, it's time to validate it with research. Market research can also provide valuable insights for enhancing your content and promotion plans. My favorite book on this topic is *Will it Fly*, by Pat Flynn. It was released in early 2016, and immediately became a #1 bestseller. Pat knows what he's doing. His book will take you through a series of tests to help you find competing products, influencers, and early adopters. One of the most valuable chapters in the book is about building a spreadsheet called a *Market Map*. Here's how to do it:

Start by creating a Google Spreadsheet with three sheets, named *Places, People,* and *Products*. Then add these three column titles to each sheet: *Name, Web Address,* and *Notes*.

This is your "Market Map," and it's where you'll record all the information you find from doing the following exercises.

Places

Let's say you want to write a book about email marketing. You'd start your research by entering search terms into Google, like this:

blog: email marketing (This tells Google to look for blogs related to email marketing)

forum: email marketing (This tells Google to look for forums related to email marketing)

site: email marketing (This tells Google to look for websites related to email marketing)

Another tip is to review the "Searches Related To" results on Google, and use them as new search terms.

In this example, we can immediately see that Constant Contact and MailChimp would be relevant companies to explore more deeply.

Social media groups are another great place to learn about your market. Search Facebook for related groups by using the same search term you used for Google, and then click the Groups tab.

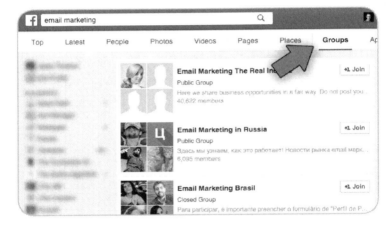

You might have to wait for an administrator to accept you into a group, so it's best to do this months in advance, before you start writing.

You'll find that Facebook groups give you a pulse on what's happening in your market. Look for groups that are active and sizable. For example, one of my favorite groups is The 7-Day Startup group, which is run by Dan Norris, author of *The 7-Day Startup*.

My books relate to startups and entrepreneurship, so this is a great fit for me. When I launched *Hustle,* I messaged the group and received a ton of great feedback (not to mention sales). As you find relevant blogs, forums, sites, and groups, add them to your *Places* sheet.

People

For the *People* sheet, search Twitter to find top influencers related to your topic.

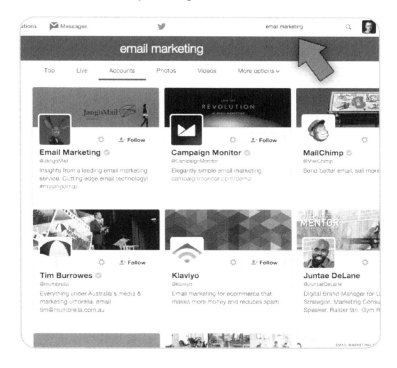

You can also use other networks, like Facebook, Instagram, Pinterest, and LinkedIn in a similar fashion. You'll often find the same people popping up across multiple networks. This is a strong indicator that you should include them on your *People* sheet!

PRO TIP

iTunes is another less obvious place to look for influencers, through podcast appearances. Once you've found a few influencers, enter their name into iTunes. If they've appeared on any podcasts, those podcasts will show up. You can then dig into those podcasts to find other people of interest. Then listen to the episodes for more information.

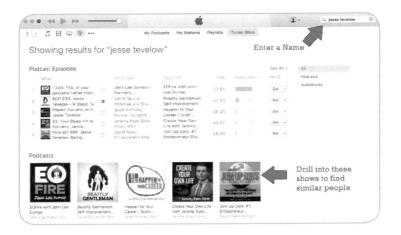

Products

For the *Products* sheet, there's one obvious place to look: Amazon. Simply enter your search term to find products related to your topic. Then drill into the books category to find direct competitors. Look at the reviews, and pay particular attention to the 2 and 3 star reviews.

Those usually contain legitimate feedback from people who liked the content on some level, but also felt that something was missing. This is key information for how you might be able to fill in the gaps with your own book.

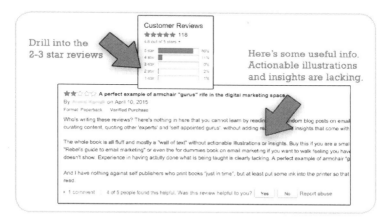

After completing these exercises and filling out your spreadsheet, you'll have a full picture of the industry surrounding your topic, and a better understanding of how to provide value to your readers. I suggest reaching out to a few of the influencers on your list and becoming active in relevant Facebook groups, too. As you get more involved with the community, you'll soak up knowledge and ultimately write a better book.

Writing: These Tricks Make It Easy

Okay, it's time to write. If this part freaks you out, don't worry. There are proven methods for easing the pain.

In fact, when using the systems below, it sometimes feels effortless. I use two techniques for attacking the blank canvas: Outlining and Dictation.

How to Build Your Outline

Writing a book is a balance between structure and flexibility. It's important to lay out your roadmap in advance, but you should also go "off script" when you find yourself in the zone.

In *Book Launch*, author Chandler Bolt describes a simple outlining technique that I've used as the basis for my process. Pat Flynn also describes a similar approach in *Will it Fly*. Here's how it works:

Step 1: Brain Dump (mind mapping). Take 30-60 minutes to write down ideas related to your book. This works best on a whiteboard, with sticky notes, or using index cards. Don't worry about grammar or organization. The content can include single words, phrases, or short sentences. You might include relevant stories from your life, tools related to your topic, a link to an article you recently read, important influencers from your Market Map spreadsheet, etc. Here's what that might look like:

The Brain Dump

IDEAS

Step 2: Sections. Now organize the content into clusters. This is really easy with sticky notes or index cards. If you used a whiteboard (or paper and pencil), you can circle things and connect them with lines and arrows. There are also several software tools for doing this, like Mindmeister.

The groupings represent potential chapters. Add titles to categorize the sections. For example, if you're writing about designing websites, the section titles might be: "Setting up Your Website," "Tools of the Trade," "Design Best Practices," etc.

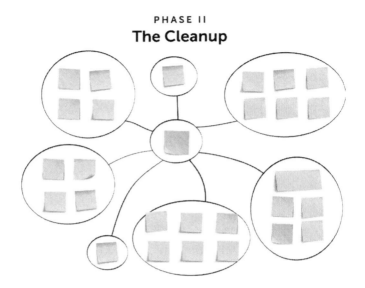

PHASE II
The Cleanup

You can also refine this further by creating ordered clusters, like this:

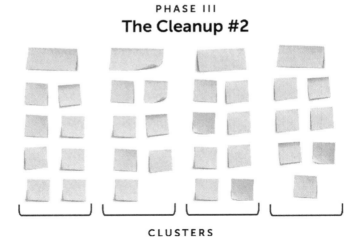

PHASE III
The Cleanup #2

CLUSTERS

Step 3: Refine, and Convert to Outline Form. For this step, you're pruning and organizing everything from steps 1 and 2. Don't be afraid to remove elements that aren't relevant.

Finally, transfer it into a manuscript document and order the sections in a way that feels logical. I use Google Docs for outlining my books. To get the exact template I use for creating my manuscripts, enroll in the free companion course here:

www.jtev.me/authorpreneur-free-course

If you're not too keen on the act of putting pen to paper, don't fret. We live in amazing times. Here are two options for dictating your book instead of writing it.

Google Docs Voice Typing
Google Docs now has a feature called voice typing. Yes, it's exactly what it sounds like. Turn on the feature (Tools > Voice Typing), start talking, and watch the words flow onto the page as you speak. It takes some practice, but once you get acclimated, it's very efficient. You can even say things like "comma" or "period" and it will assume you're talking about punctuation and add the specified symbol. I use this feature whenever I'm having a mental block. Once I have a bit of content to work from, I switch back to typing.

The Book In A Box System

Another option involving dictation is Book In A Box (BIAB). Book In A Box is a revolutionary publishing company cofounded by three-time bestselling author Tucker Max. After writing three bestsellers (the first of which was self-published until it got reprinted), Tucker found that the traditional publishing model was prohibitive for most writers. In Tucker's words, it sucks unless you're already a "media elite who lives in Manhattan."[1] The traditional publishing process can take years, and thousands of hours of commitment from the author. Book In A Box allows authors to create their book in only *twelve hours of their own time*. The process is relatively simple:

1. Create a comprehensive outline of the book
2. Dictate the outline and record it

Through transcription services, the dictation can then be easily converted to text. From there, the author can clean up the prose to make sure it reads smoothly, or hire an editor to do that.

I say this is revolutionary because it's totally different from anything we've ever done in the world of modern publishing. But it's actually not a new concept. As Tucker

---

1 https://www.youtube.com/watch?v=TI7XFtOy6MA

describes in one of his presentations about the product, dictation has been used throughout history to capture the thoughts of legends like Winston Churchill, Malcolm X, Marco Polo, Socrates, and even Jesus. If you find it difficult to structure your book, or don't like the actual process of sitting down and writing, this is a fantastic alternative. It also creates a finished product that reads as if you're speaking to the reader, which is becoming more and more popular for non-fiction books.

Tucker and his cofounder Zach Obront have published a book about their method, aptly titled: *The Book in a Box Method*. If you're considering this route, it's worth a read. I worked for BIAB as a freelance editor on a few projects, so I have an intimate understanding of their process. They provide value that's difficult to replicate. They're perfecting the outline process, building relationships with transcription services, partnering with talented editors, etc. So, if you want an experienced team who understands the intricacies of this approach, their full service package is a good idea.

Full disclosure: I have an affiliate partnership with BIAB. If you want to use their services, mention my full name as your referrer when you first sign up and you'll get a discount. It's a win-win-win. If you end up using BIAB, email me to let me know. I'd love to hear about it!

Also keep in mind, you don't necessarily need to use Book In A Box to try this method. You can also do it on your own, using their structure:

1. Create a detailed outline.
2. Dictate your story into a recorder, using the outline to direct you.
3. Transcribe the recording.
4. Polish your prose.

Proven Hacks to Improve Your Manuscript

Mention the Masters

Here's a marketing hack for you: Mention all the experts, thought-leaders, and mentors who are already established in your field within your book. This benefits you in two ways:

1. It adds credibility to your product. Established experts are seen as trusted sources. Readers will subconsciously group you with the luminaries who originally inspired your theories, and thus buy into your message with less resistance.

2. Writing about experts gives you a perfect reason to reach out to them. I used this tactic when writing *The Connection Algorithm*. I contacted everyone mentioned in the book. A handful of

them responded back, and a few even graciously offered to help me. Some of them tweeted about my book. Others, like Tony Horton and Brad Feld, gave me powerful endorsements. This type of support is priceless. It can literally take you from "just another book" to a top seller.

Hone Your Tone

Most bestselling business/lifestyle books are written with a casual tone. This is counterintuitive. In school, we're taught to use proper English. We're encouraged to use big, impressive words. But that's typically not what the masses want. The most effective technique for honing your voice is simple: mimic the voices of others. This sounds trite, but hear me out. You're not copying or imitating. You're cultivating. When you focus on a group of other voices, they all start to mix together and mesh with yours, until eventually you have something completely unique.

Some of my favorite authors include: Tim Ferriss, Malcolm Gladwell, James Altucher, Taylor Pearson, Ben Horowitz, Brad Feld, Fred Wilson (blogger), Leo Babauta, and TheMinimalists. (Note to self: I need to read more female authors). I've been reading these guys for years. Their styles influence my voice, so the end result is a mashup of the people I read, with my unique flavor at the core. It's impossible to mess this up. Your style will come out. Letting your idols rub off on you will only make it better. The more you read, the more it'll happen.

Read Aloud

This is critical. When people read your book, it should feel like you're *speaking* to them, like you're both in the same room at a dinner party. The best way to achieve this is to speak your book as you write it. It'll help you catch things that sound overly wordy or scripted. No one cares about the fancy, six-syllable word you just looked up. Use the simple, common synonym instead.

Also, keep your sentences short. People don't think in paragraphs. Shorter sentences are easier to follow.[2] Reading aloud will also help you figure out where things get too dense. Losing your reader's attention is death. You need to make sure they can keep up with you. Don't be afraid of common catch-all words, like *things, stuff, a lot*, etc. Sorry English teachers, but this is how people talk. We're not creating poetry, we're trying to engage an audience.

My loose technique is to write a few paragraphs and then read them aloud. I don't break my writing flow, I

---

2 Read this brilliant article by Scott Adams (creator of Dilbert) for a quick lesson on effective writing: https://tinyurl.com/o7ubfk6

just stop whenever it feels natural. When reading aloud, I make edits whenever something sounds awkward or forced. When a chapter is complete, I do the same thing for the entire chapter. This process continues until absolutely *nothing* in the book trips me up, from start to finish. It's tedious, but if you follow through with it, you'll end up with an engaging, easy-to-read book.

How Many Hours of Work Per Day?

I like what Woody Allen says about productivity: "If you work only three to five hours a day, you become very productive. It's the steadiness of it that counts. Getting to the typewriter every day is what makes productivity."[3] I find this to be amazingly true. If I can make solid progress for three to five hours per day, I'm highly productive. It becomes a problem only if I skip days (outside of weekends). The key is to keep the momentum going. Avoiding burnout is a critical part of that. Slow and steady wins the race.

Three to five hours might sound like it's not enough, but consider that you can write 1,000 words per hour if you're inspired and motivated. That gets you to about 40,000 words (a roughly 200 page book) in ten days, or two weeks if we don't include weekends. Of course you'll need to do outlining and research

---

3 Taken from an excerpt of James Altucher's *Choose Yourself*.

throughout the process, so let's add in another forty hours for those tasks. At an average of four hours per day, that's still only another ten business days, or another two weeks. The book would be done in a month. This is purely hypothetical and admittedly unrealistic since 4,000 words per day is typically not a sustainable pace over time, but it's a good demonstration of how consistency leads to ultra-productivity.

Allow Randomness and Break the Rules

As I've mentioned, sometimes I don't follow my routine at all. Some nights, I write until 3 a.m. If you find yourself in a state of intense motivation, don't fight it—flow with it. Your best material will come in these moments, when you're in the Zone.

There's a critical distinction between a *rule* and a *law*. A law can't be broken. A rule, on the other hand, can and *should* be broken if it benefits you (and doesn't hurt anyone else). Your daily routine is important because it establishes the general rules around getting things done. But don't be afraid of breaking those rules if it works in your favor.

Cut the Fluff

There's no correct length for a book, but most non-fiction books fall into the 30–60K word range. *The Connection Algorithm* was around 50K. This book is shorter. I'm mentioning this simply to give you a benchmark. Don't fill your book with fluff to hit a desired page count or word count. That definitely won't help your sales.

Tucker Max gave a talk at The Next Web conference about the book industry.[4] He argued that a 150 page book is actually superior to a 300 page book. Why? Because people find long books daunting. He also explained that books have historically averaged between 250-300 pages, mainly because publishing companies know that creating a spine wide enough to clearly show the title helps the book sell more copies in bookstores. This is clearly an archaic strategy for determining the optimal length of a book.

Build Your Toolbox

I use Google Docs for my actual manuscript. I format my documents to resemble a true print version. This helps me visualize how the book will feel, and helps me find good paragraph breaks (which I keep short in most cases). Formatting your document isn't mandatory and most publishers discourage it, but I find it helpful. To see a downloadable manuscript template, view the resources found in the free companion course here:

www.jtev.me/authorpreneur-free-course

---

4 https://youtu.be/TI7XFtOy6MA

I've heard good things about Scrivener, but haven't used it. To store random notes, I use Evernote (www.evernote.com). To bookmark relevant articles or websites, I use Pocket (www.getpocket.com). For general project management and goal-setting, I use Asana (www.asana.com) and Trello (www.trello.com).

The 30-Day Authorpreneur Challenge

The biggest speed bump stopping people from completing a project is *a failure to start*. Don't let that be you. Instead, hit the ground running and make yourself accountable. You can do that by joining the *Authorpreneur* Facebook group. It's simple. Join the group and make a commitment to write content for your book for 30 days in a row. There's no word count requirement—just write *something* each day. Post in the group daily with your current streak (i.e. "Day 1-30"), your word count for that day, and your total word count for the challenge. And feel free to chat with other members of the group for support. You'd be surprised how much it can help.

Request to join the private group here:

https://www.facebook.com/groups
/AuthorpreneurGroup/

TL;DR, Resources, and Next Steps

TL;DR (Summary)

- Choosing your #1 goal is the first step in the writing process. Your strategy will change depending on your goal.

- You should price your book either high or low, depending on the goal (above)

- There are three approaches to finding a topic:
  › Explain how to do something.
  › Offer a strong opinion relating to a trend.
  › Tell an interesting story.

- To narrow your focus, use the Who, What, Why method.

- Use the Three "P" Market Research method to gain insights on your book's topic.

- Structuring your book before you write is extremely important. It can be done in three steps:
  › Brain Dump
  › Sections
  › Refinement

- Use dictation if you find writing from scratch to be a challenge.

- These writing techniques will improve your finished product:
  › Mentioning the masters
  › Honing your tone
  › Reading your draft aloud
  › Maintaining a schedule
  › Allowing randomness
  › Cutting the fluff

Resources

The full set of resources for this chapter can be found in the Authorpreneur Companion Course. To get the free course and materials, go here:

www.jtev.me/authorpreneur-free-course

Next Steps

Following these guidelines will result in an engaging book that will effectively serve a targeted audience. But let's take it a step further. The highest performing books have two other things in common.

1. They're promoted well
2. They look amazing

DR. GARETH THOMPSON

Gareth Thompson started his adult life as a doctor, but then decided to go back to business school for an MBA. He was clearly driven. But he was unsure of the path he wanted to travel. Post-MBA, Gareth toyed with various ideas for new inventions and companies. Eventually, his vision crystallized into a concept that could serve all his interests equally: He would build an army of entrepreneur-innovators to solve some of the world's toughest problems, starting with the environment.

While all of this was happening, Gareth came to an

important realization. As entrepreneurship becomes more prevalent, navigating an MBA program and deciding what to do with it is more nebulous than ever before. But it's still incredibly valuable. There's a new type of graduate emerging from business schools—*The MBA Entrepreneur*.

This became the title of Gareth's first book. It recounts his journey through the MBA system and seeks to offer actionable advice to others who might be considering an MBA or deciding what to do with their degree. After working with LaunchTeam, Gareth described our process as a life-changing experience. He was able to achieve bestseller status on Amazon and can now use the book to position himself as an expert as he continues his adventures in medicine, entrepreneurship, and innovation.

Here's how Gareth describes the experience: "Simon and Jesse helped me to completely transform my book. The raw manuscript contained a lot of valuable insights, but it was unfocused. With their help, I repositioned the book with a new title, a new cover, a tighter manuscript, and a laser targeted aim. The end result was a book that went from being an interesting story to a book that would help both myself and the reader to build a career in entrepreneurship. It was 1,000x better."

Want to launch your own book? You can join the free Authorpreneur Companion Course to download our launch materials and learn more about our process.

www.jtev.me/authorpreneur-free-course

CHAPTER 6

MARKETING & DESIGN

The Biggest Mistake Amateur Authors Make

The importance of design and marketing can't be understated, yet most self-published authors neglect it. Remember, 50% (or more) of your time needs to be spent on gaining traction, and design and marketing are the two biggest factors in that equation.

Design is one of the few areas where traditional publishers still have an edge over self-publishers. But that's only because the majority of self-published authors don't spend the time or money investing in good design. All it takes is a little effort. Design encompasses all aspects of the reader's experience. This includes the interior layout, typography, interior graphics, front matter, back matter, cover/jacket design, the selected materials for paperback/hardcover versions—and even the content itself. Remember that marketing considerations should play into the book's design, too. You can certainly learn how to do all of this on your own, but I recommend hiring contractors. You'll save time and likely end up with a better result.

Market Within Your Book

Once you're a published author on Amazon, you'll have immediate access to the millions of people searching Amazon every day. The beginning of your book (which can be read for free using the "Look Inside" feature on Amazon) presents a valuable marketing opportunity. Add call-to-action links at the beginning and end of your book to direct people to your email list signup page. The call-to-action will drive new traffic to your landing pages and capture more list subscribers—even if they don't purchase your book!

To entice readers, you can provide a link to free resources. Examples include email templates, project plan templates, further reading lists, useful links, etc. Compile all of this information online and allow readers to access it only after providing their email address. This can be done using software like Leadpages, Unbounce, or ConvertKit. These are paid services, but I highly recommend them. Remember, collecting emails allows you to sell other products more effectively in the future.

PRO TIP

You can also create a free companion course to collect emails, and then house all the resources within the course. This is the method I've used for Authorpreneur.

Reach out to Podcasters

In 2007, Tim Ferriss famously went to a conference called South By Southwest (SXSW) to meet bloggers and tell them about his first book, *The Four Hour Workweek*. He created lasting relationships at the conference, and was able to befriend big-name bloggers who eventually agreed to promote his book during his launch.

Tim has said this was one of his secret weapons for topping the bestseller charts. Traditional forms of promotion, like online marketing, weren't moving the needle, but being featured on a blog with a targeted readership increased sales significantly. In 2007, blogging was relatively new. It was an untapped market and it was full of people who liked to read. Today, blogging is saturated. The new frontier is podcasting. With the abundance of mobile phones, podcasting has exploded as a highly personal way to reach large, targeted audiences. People are listening to podcasts during their workouts, around the house, and while commuting to and from work.

I didn't schedule any podcast appearances for my first book, which was a big mistake. You should definitely use this strategy for your launch. You'll want to schedule interviews in conjunction with a free promo on the first few days of your book's official release. Look for podcasts that relate to your book's content. A good site for searching podcasts is podbay.fm.

You might get turned down, but that's okay. You can still succeed without podcast appearances (I didn't have any to start). And if your book does well after its launch, you can reach out again. Once a podcaster sees some validation in the market, they'll be more likely to invite you to appear on their show. In your podcast interviews, refer to your book and mention the link to your landing page. You can even create customized landing pages for each podcast interview.[1]

Invest in Book Design

While writing your book, reach out to a book designer.
There's a lot to know about designing a book. There
are all kinds of standard styles and conventions for
fonts, spacing, quotes, margins, etc. I recommend creating versions of your book in the following formats:

ePub - Standard file for digital book reading
devices.

mobi - Standard file for Amazon Kindle books.

PDF (Standard) - Good for sending to people for
free. Still works on computers, and most phones
and tablets.

PDF (CreateSpace) - This is the format required
by CreateSpace (a company owned by Amazon) to
publish your book in paperback format. They have
exact specifications on their website.

---

1 Here's the ultimate guide to getting featured on podcasts,
courtesy of Taylor Pearson: https://tinyurl.com/ya35bmrp

Note: If there's one thing to spend money on besides marketing, this is it. For your book to reach a mainstream audience, it needs to look professional. An entire soup-to-nuts design will likely cost you a few thousand dollars, but it's money well spent. A few options for that include Winning Edits and The Frontispiece. Alternatively, you can look for designers on design/freelance sites like Reedsy, Dribbble, Behance, or 99designs. Doing a quick search for 'book designer' also turns up some options.

> **PRO TIP**
> Creating a hardcover version is unnecessary. I spent $5,000 doing this for my first book and it wasn't worth it. Amazon can create high-quality paperbacks on demand, so you can still offer a physical version (which adds validity and creates opportunities for price differentiation), without spending money on production up front.

Get an Editor

I categorize every aspect of the user experience as design work. Editors craft your content. They make it more visually appealing by improving your prose, not only from a syntax perspective, but also from a content perspective. This is usually two separate jobs done by two different people:

A *copy editor* is focused on grammar, punctuation, and sentence structure.

A *content editor* will dig into your material and suggest conceptual edits to make it better. This might include identifying logic-gaps, commenting on the book's structure and pacing, and questioning your assumptions. They'll also view your book from a marketing perspective to ensure the final output will be palatable (and useful) for your intended audience.

I recommend hiring both types of editors. Elisa Doucette and her team at Craft Your Content has been highly recommended by several bestselling author friends of mine. CYC has a team of both content editors *and* copy editors. Winning Edits is another incredibly strong team that can do everything from interior and exterior design, to graphics, content editing, and more. On the higher end of the pricing spectrum for content editing, you can try Command+Z Content, run by Nils Parker and Ann Maynard. Their firm has produced a number of bestsellers for big name authors.

How to Find Contractors

To find other contractors a-la-carte, try searching a marketplace service like Reedsy. They have a good database of talented freelancers who do everything from copy-editing to cover design.

Choose a Title That Doesn't Suck

Our standard formula for titles is to use a short, catchy title followed by a longer subtitle that plainly states the book's value proposition. Don't get fancy with this. Your title (along with the descriptive subtitle) should be crystal clear. It should never leave prospective readers guessing about the content.

Examples:

Sprint: How to Solve Big Problems and Test New Ideas in Just Five Days

Will it Fly? How to Test Your Next Business Idea So You Don't Waste Your Time and Money

The Power of Habit: Why We Do What We Do in Life and Business

Living Forward: A Proven Plan to Stop Drifting and Get the Life You Want

Traction: How Any Startup Can Achieve Explosive Customer Growth

Of course there are other successful books that don't follow this structure, but this is what I see most often. To see other successful nonfiction titles, go to Amazon and browse the bestseller lists within the business categories, like this:

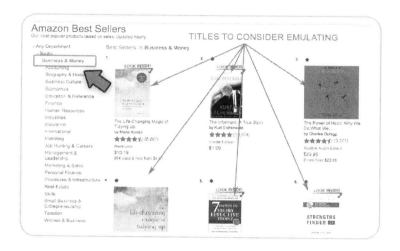

TL;DR, Resources, and Next Steps

TL;DR (Summary)

- One of the last remaining differentiators between traditionally published and self-published books is design. If you design your book well and hire the right people to help you, readers won't be able to distinguish your self-published book from a traditionally published book.

- You should put a link to capture leads in the front of your book. This will keep the marketing flywheel spinning for future products.

- Reach out to podcasters to see if you can be a guest on their show. Podcasting is a highly efficient way to get free marketing and exposure.

- Invest in book design for both the interior design and the cover.

- Get a copy editor and a content editor. They're usually two different people.

- Choose a title that doesn't suck by looking at other popular titles. The main title should be short and catchy. The subtitle should be descriptive.

Resources

The full set of resources for this chapter can be found in the Authorpreneur Companion Course. To get the free course and materials, go here:

www.jtev.me/authorpreneur-free-course

Next Steps

After your book is written, edited, and professionally designed, it's time to prep for the launch and build some early buzz. Lucky for you, that's the topic of the following chapter.

KATIE SOY

Katie Soy has a vision. She plans to write multiple books, including a trilogy. She writes fiction stories, and her first title, *The Fenix Projects,* is already available online and in bookstores. It's a gripping thriller, giving us a glimpse into the dark world of human sex trafficking in the northwest United States. The book is based on true events and it reads like a movie script, which is no accident. There are hopes that her stories and characters might travel to the big screen someday.

Regardless, Katie's first book has already been a huge success. Working with her publisher, LifeStyle

Entrepreneurs Press, we helped Katie hit #1 on Amazon and get over 100 customer reviews. *The Fenix Projects* is also now being distributed in bookstores across America.

The really cool part about this is that Katie worked with LaunchTeam in various capacities after her launch, helping others achieve similar results with *their* books. She also plans on using her storytelling skills to create new consulting services that will supplement book sales. This is a perfect example of how a fiction author can still employ marketing and business tactics to create new opportunities around their book.

Katie said, "Working with Jesse and Simon at Launchteam for my first book was one of the best choices I made during the launch. They invested their time and energy into my story coming into the world as if it was their own. They break down the overwhelming launch process into easy, doable steps and offered guidance and coaching when I needed advice or had questions. They were extremely influential in my book hitting #1 in my desired category and additional top categories on Amazon. Their expertise was so valuable and they run their business with kindness and integrity. Their encouragement and professionalism were much needed in my first-time-author journey, and I look forward to working with them in the future."

Want to launch your own book? You can join the free Authorpreneur Companion Course to download our launch materials and learn more about our process.

www.jtev.me/authorpreneur-free-course

CHAPTER 7

BUILD BUZZ & PREPARE FOR LIFTOFF

Completing a full-length manuscript and designing the final product certainly takes focus, attention, and hard work, but it's critical to put just as much effort into preparing for the launch itself. Don't forget this part!

Set Up a Giveaway

One way to start building buzz for your book is to run a giveaway for other similar books in anticipation of your title's forthcoming release. KingSumo is a tool for creating viral giveaways. To sign up for the give-away, people must submit their email address. You can include your book, along with other items, as a prize. Or, as mentioned, you can simply give away books that are similar to your book. This will ensure you're attracting the right kind of people to your list. (For example, you wouldn't want to attract soccer moms if your target audience is college students. So, select your prizes accordingly.)

KingSumo is valuable because it supercharges your social media efforts. People are far more likely to share something if it's free, and if it involves prizes. Furthermore, because of KingSumo's unique sharing design, people are incentivized to invite their friends.

Selling Platforms: Amazon, or Direct Pay?

For list-building and distribution, Amazon is the best choice, simply because their platform is so massive. That said, it also takes a little more work because you'll distribute through both Kindle (digital) and CreateSpace (paperback). Sign up for both Kindle and CreateSpace. (FYI, both services are owned by Amazon). This will make your book available in both digital and paperback formats for your launch, with-out costing anything up front, except for a few small things like obtaining an ISBN.

The process is relatively straightforward. The

details for creating a cover and manuscript file can be found on their site. Send those specs to your designer. After receiving the formatted files from your designer, upload them to your CreateSpace account. CreateSpace will assign an ISBN (barcode) to your book. Set your price, which can be changed at any time in the future, and add the same description you created for your Kindle version. Then submit it for review. The review will take a few days. Finally, order a proof of your book. CreateSpace will mail it to you within a week or so. If the proof looks good, you're all set to offer paperbacks on launch day.

Important: When you sign up for Kindle, make sure you enroll in KDP Select. This will allow you to launch your book with a price tag of $0.00 for the first few days. This is key because:

1. **People love free.** A bunch of people will download your book due to the $0.00 price tag. And guess what? If you follow my guidelines correctly, those customers will still be incredibly valuable because they'll notice the call-to-action on your opening pages and a percentage of them will convert to list subscribers, which means you can sell them other useful products and services down the road.

2. **Launching for free is the only way to deliver on the promise you made** to people who subscribed to your email list before the book was published. (Yes, you could send a PDF, but giving them access to the actual Kindle version is much better.)

How to Optimize Amazon Categories

On Amazon, you can choose up to two categories for your book. You want to choose categories that are relevant, but not overly saturated with high-performing titles. Essentially, you want to find categories in which you can compete. You don't want to be going up against Malcolm Gladwell's bestseller in the #1 spot. So, find a category where the #1 spot is held by a book with a low ranking. To find good categories:

1. Go to Amazon and click into the Kindle Store. On the left, you'll see categories.
2. Start perusing the categories to find ones that look relevant to your book.
3. Click into a category and go to the sales page of the #1 book. Scroll down and look for the overall ranking.
4. Add the ranking into a spreadsheet and keep a running list. After you've searched 20–30 categories, you'll have a good sense of your best options.

To see how I did this with my first book, view the free resources at the end of the chapter.

Add Descriptions, Keywords, and Subtitles
You'll need to fill out a bunch of form fields to create your sales page on Amazon. A few of the important fields are: Book Description, Keywords, and Subtitle.

You should spend considerable time crafting your book's description. It's a big factor in sales, both algorithmically and in terms of customer perception. Keywords should be included in the description. For example, if your book is about taking risks, you should include words like "risk" and "risk-taking." There's a separate section where you can include up to seven additional keywords. Again, choose words that are relevant to your book. Finally, you can include a subtitle. This is an opportunity to add more search terms with high volume.

I use a tool called MerchantWords for finding good keywords. It allows you to enter search terms, and then returns the number of queries for those terms on Amazon. By selecting high-volume terms, your book will theoretically appear more often in organic searches. You can also find books with good descriptions by using the same strategy I mentioned for crafting a title:

Go to Amazon and browse the bestsellers in the business category. Find a book that matches the style of your book, and then mimic the layout and content of their book description. For example, for my first book, *The Connection Algorithm*, I mimicked Tim Ferriss' description for *The Four Hour Workweek*.

Set Up Your Amazon Author Page
Amazon allows you to create an author page that links to your books. Upload a professional photo, along with a bio. Once you fill out your author page, the photo and bio will appear on your sales page, along with an author ranking based on your book's sales. This makes your Amazon sales page look far more professional.

Set Up Your Own Sales Page
If you don't use Amazon for distribution, I'd recommend setting up your own sales page and selling independently. Good direct-payment services include SamCart, ThriveCart, or Gumroad. Many authors are finding success with this, earning impressive revenue since they don't need to split the pie with a distributor. Be careful, though. This method only works well if you already have a large following or know how to optimize the SEO of your site and drive traffic to it.

Here are some independent sales page examples:

- www.nathanbarry.com/authority
- http://personalmba.com/
- https://designcode.io/

Share Everywhere

When your book launches, you need to notify as much of the internet as possible. There are obvious places like Facebook and Twitter where you can message your friends and fans, but you should look for new communities as well. A good one is Product Hunt. You should sign up at least a month in advance. It requires membership or an invite from an existing member before you can post content. This is just one example. Look for others.

Get Pre-Launch Reviews

Remember how I suggested you should create a Facebook group to build a community of fans who are interested in your book, or create a group using LaunchTeam? That's because you can leverage those people for important launch efforts, like getting early reviews. You should send PDF versions of your book to your launch team members. Ask them to read some of the book and prepare a quick review *before* you officially launch on Amazon. Let people know it's part of your launch strategy. If people feel involved with your plan, they'll be more excited to help you. If you have any high-profile friends, ask them to send you a short quote you can add to your editorial review section on Amazon. My company, LaunchTeam, uses a specific process for obtaining early reviews. If you're interested in learning more, join the free *Authorpreneur* Companion Course.

www.jtev.me/authorpreneur-free-course

The Week Before Launch

Here's what you should do during the week leading up to your launch.

1. **Upload your book file to Amazon.** Three to five days prior to launch is the sweet spot for uploading your digital book file to Amazon and publishing it. If you publish too far in advance of your actual launch, you're cutting into your exposure on the 'Hot New Releases' list (Amazon will only feature it for up to 30 days from the time the file is uploaded). If you upload too close to your launch date, the book file might not get processed in time.[1]

---

1 Hat tip to Chandler Bolt on this.

2. **Email Your Team.** The day before the launch, email your entire list and your launch team members again, reminding them that the book will be free for the next few days. Also remind them to post their review.

TL;DR, Resources, and Next Steps

TL;DR (Summary)

- Run a giveaway to generate buzz and collect more emails for your launch.

- If your goal is list-building or brand building, you should launch on Amazon. If you want to generate more income, you can consider a high price, direct pay model using a payment service like SamCart or ThriveCart.

- Sign up for sites that offer product distribution, like Product Hunt.

- Get pre-launch reviews from your early adopters and launch team members.

- The week before launch, upload your book file to Amazon and email your lists to prep them for launch week.

Resources

The full set of resources for this chapter can be found in the Authorpreneur Companion Course. To get the free course and materials, go here:

www.jtev.me/authorpreneur-free-course

Next Steps

Now that you've included all the proper marketing hooks in your book, settled on a title, set your pricing, set up your sales pages, and optimized your book description—it's time to launch (and sell!)

PREDICTABLE RESULTS

Rhythm Systems is a company that helps other mid-market businesses achieve better results through a combination of software, proven methodologies, and expert consultation. The team at Rhythm Systems wanted to demonstrate the predictable results they're able to achieve through their various services and philosophies, so they set out to write a book about it. They called it Predictable Results. The book has nine authors, all of whom bring their unique experience to the discussion.

After enlisting LaunchTeam to help with the

marketing and launch efforts, the book soared to #1 in multiple categories on Amazon within the first week and amassed over 75 customer reviews. The company is now able to use the book as the foundation of their brand.

Here's what Barry Pruitt, our main contact from Rhythm Systems, had to say about the project: "Wow! Confusion, anxiety, nine authors, and two stakeholders. As the main author contact, I found that things changed often on our end, but Jesse, Simon, and team handled us masterfully. We advise our clients to 'trust the process' because it's been proven over and over. When LaunchTeam told me to trust the process, I had to laugh at myself. I felt exactly what my new clients feel. LaunchTeam was not only empathetic, they were right! Their process works."

Want to launch your own book? You can join the free Authorpreneur Companion Course to download our launch materials and learn more about our process.

www.jtev.me/authorpreneur-free-course

 CHAPTER 8

LAUNCH & SELL

Free Promo

I mentioned that when you set up your Amazon page, you should select KDP Select. One of the perks of KDP Select is the ability to run free promo days. You're allowed to offer your book for free for up to five days per 90-day enrollment period. I recommend running 3-5 promo days in a row as part of your initial launch strategy. Running a free promo at launch will help boost your sales (people like free books). When your book moves up the free charts, it will start showing up in other areas of Amazon's site, such as "Hot New Releases" and "Customers Who Bought This Item Also Bought."

The paid list and the free list are exclusive, but when you switch from free to paid, all of the product placement you achieved from your free promo will stay intact for a few hours. This will lead to organic paid sales, which will improve your paid ranking, which will keep your book visible in the special promo sections. This is why reaching a high ranking during your free promo is so important for sustained sales after converting to paid. It can literally determine your book's success or failure.

Note: If you reach the top 100 free books, you're in great shape. Amazon highlights the top 100, which means tens of thousands of eyeballs. If this happens, you should manually stop your promo during primetime hours (12-5PM EST). This will ensure you get the most paid sales possible when you make the switch from free to paid.

> **PRO TIP**
>
> In all of your communications with fans and friends, say your promo will only last for two days. This gives you the opportunity to manually stop the promo if you reach the top 100, which allows you to save three of your five promo days for later. If the promo isn't going so well, it gives you another excuse to contact people again with the good news that the promo period has been extended.

The Four Phases of a Launch

We have a four-phase process for launching books. Phase one begins on a Friday. This is our soft launch. For the soft launch, we hit the 'publish' button on Amazon, but we don't promote it publicly. Instead, we email our launch team members and ask them to post their reviews over the weekend. This way, the book has a bunch of reviews by Monday. On Monday, we enter phase two, which is our free promo period. During this phase, we post in relevant Facebook groups and a few other locations to move up the free charts. On Tuesday, we move into phase three, our paid promo period. During this phase, we change the price of the book to

$0.99, which is when the bulk of our promotion drops. This is the official 'launch day.' Tuesday onward is phase four, which is for ongoing marketing and promotion (the phase that never ends). This process is explained in more detail in a comprehensive video that can be accessed from the Companion Course.

www.jtev.me/authorpreneur-free-course

Promote. Promote. Promote.
You should promote your book like a maniac during your free days. Understandably, people are much more willing to download a free book than a paid book. Your friends will also be more willing to promote a free product to their networks. Focus on Facebook, email lists, and launch team members. If you have any pre-recorded podcasts, this is also the best time to release them.

Twitter is overrated for promo (unless you have a massive or highly-targeted following that will be interested in your book). The signal-to-noise ratio is too low. That said, I do have a list of Twitter handles that promote free books. You can tweet at them, but don't spend too much time on it. For a list of Facebook groups where you can post about your book, relevant Twitter accounts to tweet at, and some other goodies, access the free Companion Course and download the resources.

The Selling Never Stops

You've put a lot of work into building your platform, writing your book, designing it, and launching it. But your work isn't done. Selling is never-ending, which means you need to keep marketing as well. Book reviews make your sales page more impressive, which leads to more paying customers. There are several hacks for increasing reviews, and a few to avoid.

Follow up With Fans via Twitter

Within your book (toward the end), ask people to tweet at you if they enjoyed it. When someone tweets at you, they'll likely follow you. If you follow them back, you can send direct messages. Send them a note, politely asking them to leave a review. Provide them with a link to the review page to remove as much friction as possible. To download a templated set of messages that are proven to work, access the free Companion Course and download the resources. (I've used this method to get hundreds of authentic reviews for my own books.)

> **PRO TIP**
> Put the tweet request before your acknowledgements section. Amazon often hides the acknowledgements and takes readers directly to an exit page instead, so most people won't see it if you put it in the acknowledgements or anywhere after that.

Contact Super Reviewers

There are super reviewers who write Amazon reviews professionally. Many of them are speed readers. You can find ranked lists here:

- http://www.amazon.com/review/hall-of-fame
- http://www.amazon.com/review/top-reviewers/

You can also find some good tips by Googling "amazon top book reviewers." I used these methods to get reviews for *The Connection Algorithm* from several hall-of-fame reviewers, which helped my review ranking and also allowed me to add their remarks as editorial reviews.

Avoid Review Exchanges

There are review exchanges where authors leave reviews for eachother, but I don't recommend using them. You'll end up with reviews that aren't genuine, which can work against you. The number of reviews matters, but the quality and authenticity matter more.

Offer a Prize to Readers

This is a method I've seen employed by other best-selling authors:

1. Email everyone who already purchased the book and gave you their email address. If you don't have a list, try using Facebook or other social channels.
2. Explain that you're giving away a prize. A good option might be books that are similar to yours, or an Amazon gift card.
3. Provide the link to leave a review and explain that you appreciate honest reviews, but that clicking the link will enter them into the contest to win the prize even if they don't leave a review. (That last part is important).
4. Explain that the contest only lasts for a few days.
5. On the last day of the contest, remind people again with another email.
6. Watch the reviews roll in!
7. After the contest is over, use your email marketing provider to download the list of people

who clicked the link. Then use a random number generator (for example: https://www.random.org/) to generate a number within that range and identify a winner.

8. Email the winner and deliver their prize!

Note: Incentivizing reviews is against Amazon's TOS. This method is still okay because everyone is eligible to receive the prize, even if they don't leave a review.

Increasing Visibility

Goodreads is a popular website for book recommendations and reviews. It's a community of millions. You can add your book to Goodreads and join their authors program for free, which gives you an upgraded account with extra features. From there, you can advertise your book, create promotional giveaways, or simply participate in discussions and rate other books to engage with the community. This is just one more simple way to add more validity around your book and distribute it to a wider audience. People use Goodreads as a source of credibility, so acquiring positive reviews on their site is just as valuable as Amazon reviews.

Paid Advertising

When I launched my first book, I spent around $100 on Facebook and Amazon ads. Even though this didn't contribute to a noticeable amount of sales, it had the benefit of bumping my rankings, which may have contributed to organic sales through search. During our launches, we often do a small amount of advertising on Facebook and/or Amazon to drive sales on our initial launch day. We don't use it as a monetization strategy because the math typically doesn't work.

Note: If you're using the High-Value Niche Market Method, this type of advertising becomes more viable long-term. With a higher price point (let's say $150) and no middle-man, you can spend more money on advertising, knowing you'll get your money back even if only a small percentage of people convert on your ad. A typical cost-per-click on a good Facebook ad is $0.50. If the conversion from click-throughs to purchase is 1%, and 100 people click my ad, I just spent $50 for those 100 clicks, but I earned $150 on the sale, so I made $100.

If my book was priced on Amazon for something much lower, let's say $10, I would have made $7 on the sale ($3 goes to Amazon) and spent $50 on the ads, losing $43 overall. The high price point flips the equation from unprofitable to profitable. This is another benefit of the niche model. You can also create this same effect by using a sales funnel. This means there's another service or product tied to the book on the backend. This book is an example of that, because we offer services at LaunchTeam that are mentioned in the book.

Post-Launch Pricing Strategies

Amazon permits you to price your book between $2.99–$9.99 with a 70% royalty, or $0.99-$200.00 with a 35% royalty (yeah, it's weird, but that's how it works). When I first started, my sweet spot for maximizing units-sold *and* profit was $2.99. If I went over 2.99, my sales would drop. If I went below 2.99, sales would increase, but I would earn less at a lower percentage royalty. As you become more established, you can charge more, but if you're a first-time author, I recommend starting with $0.99 when you switch from free to paid. This will optimize your ranking, which should be your initial focus.

When you have more than one version of your book available, Amazon shows the full price of the print version on the Kindle page, crossed off. So I use the paperback or hardcover version to create the illusion of a deep discount on the Kindle version. It looks like this:

Print List Price: ~~$14.99~~
Kindle Price: $0.99
Save $14.00 (93%)

People love to feel like they're getting a deal. It creates the perception of saving money. By pricing the hard-copy high and the Kindle version low, I push everyone to buy the digital version—so my sales are focused (as opposed to distributed), which maximizes my Kindle rankings. My overarching recommendation with pricing is to optimize for volume over profit in the early days. Your goal should be to climb the rankings, not to fill your bank account. Once you've exhausted all options for climbing the rankings, you can start optimizing for profit.

Appear as a Guest on Podcasts

Podcasts are one of the best ways to achieve ongoing exposure for your book. Once the book is written, it becomes an obvious marketing tool and an easy pitch for you to appear on relevant podcast shows. You can reach out to podcast hosts directly, or use a service to do this for you. For example, my company has a PR department focused entirely on booking clients for appearances on podcasts (and across other media outlets).

Create an Audio Version of Your Book

An audio version of your book can increase sales and exposure. If you want to retain the rights to the audio version, create it on your own and offer it outside of the major distribution platforms (i.e. don't list it on

Amazon). This can be valuable if you want to give your audio version away for free. A popular strategy is to offer the audio version for free in the beginning of the digital and print versions of the book. This becomes a lead magnet for you to collect more emails for your email list. If you aren't concerned with ownership or using the audio version as a lead magnet, just use Amazon's audio company, Audible.

Earning "Passive" Income

Passive income isn't really passive. You can't write a book, publish it, and then watch TV while the book makes you rich. There's always work to be done; it just shifts into broader and broader categories as you build out your brand or company. At first, you're working directly on the book. Then you're working on launching the book. Then you're working on promoting the book. Then you're working on promoting your brand or business. Each of these elements gets further and further away from working on the actual book. But each element still greatly affects your sales, and has secondary effects for your bottom line.

The Four Hour Workweek, by Tim Ferriss, is one of the most successful books of all time in terms of sales. It was on the bestseller list for nearly a decade. In part, this is because the book is really good, so it spreads through word of mouth. But it's also because

Tim Ferriss is constantly promoting himself as a brand, which indirectly leads to sales of *The Four Hour Workweek,* along with all his other products. If Tim had written the book and then hid in a cave for the rest of his life, his sales wouldn't be anywhere near where they are today.

So yes, the work on the actual product becomes passive, but your work in general still needs to remain active. The good news is that whatever you decide to do next (as long as it's visible to the world) should naturally contribute to your sales. Tim doesn't need to focus on selling *The Four Hour Workweek* anymore. He can focus on his latest projects, which strengthens his brand, which then indirectly drives more sales to the original book.

Don't Ignore What You Can't Measure

If we don't measure ourselves and our work, we have no basis for comparison, and therefore no way of tracking improvement. When I worked in the game industry, I always kept my eye on the major players, hoping to learn from them. One of the powerhouses at the time was Zynga. They were one of the first purely social gaming companies, born out of the Facebook platform. Zynga was notorious for being a data driven company. They were often called a data analytics company disguised as a game company. In the early days of Zynga, it appeared that every decision was based

"What gets measured gets managed."

—PETER DRUCKER

on data. They used data to *drive* decisions vs. letting it *inform* their decisions. They didn't care about the unmeasurable elements of their games, like the quality of the artwork or the creativity of the game mechanics.

Zynga went public in 2011. Their market cap quickly ballooned to $10 billion, but a few months later, they started losing users. Within the first year in the public markets, their value fell over 80%, to around $2 billion.[1] Then employees started leaving. Why? Not because of the plunge in market value. It was something far *less* measurable than that: An undesirable culture.

Zynga grew, in large part, by acquisition. They would buy successful teams and plug them into the 'Zynga machine.' Zynga's culture was defined by long hours and speedy outputs, much like an investment bank. This makes sense if you know the history of Mark Pincus, the company's CEO. Before starting Zynga, he worked as an investment banker on Wall Street—so he ran Zynga the same way. In fact, he was known to poach investment bankers as a hiring strategy, placing them into executive roles to help manage his data driven company. "Work at Zynga Speed" was one of their values.

If you know any investment bankers, they usually don't last more than a few years, which creates a very

---

1 https://tinyurl.com/y9x7tyst

fragile culture. As Zynga lost momentum in the public markets, employees were also burning out. Without a rich culture to stabilize them, they fled. Other game companies with a much slower and more deliberate approach (like Supercell and King) eventually pulled ahead, even though they had fewer employees who worked fewer hours.

Zynga was also forgetting a key element of the gaming world—fun. Games are supposed to create joy, not just profit. Zynga placed too much value on what they could measure, and not enough on what they *couldn't* measure. To thrive, you need to address *both*. It's true that "What gets measured gets managed." But here's an equally profound corollary: "What can't be measured often matters most."

Let me bring this back to center. Can you measure the effect of talking to your Uber driver about your book while you head to your destination? Can you measure the effect of the review you left on *someone else's book*, or the detailed answer you gave on Quora relating to your book's topic? Can you measure whether or not a thoughtful tweet pulled someone into your digital sphere and eventually lead them to purchase your book? Can you measure the effect of your tone and passion when you write? Can you measure the relationship between the quality of your book's content and its sales? No. You can't measure any of those things. *But they all matter.*

TL;DR, Resources, and Next Steps

TL;DR (Summary)

- You should launch with KDP's free option. Make your book free for the first 3-5 days of your launch.

- Launch on a Tuesday, but use our four phase process (which actually starts on the Friday prior).

- During launch week, post to Facebook, Twitter, and product sites like Product Hunt.

- After launch week, the selling doesn't stop. It's a constant pursuit. There are various things you can do to improve sales, including:

  › Post-launch review hacks
  › Increasing visibility with established communities like Goodreads
  › Advertising with paid ad campaigns
  › Playing with pricing
  › Appearing on podcasts
  › Creating an audio version

- Passive income is never completely passive. It still takes work if you expect to optimize it.

- Don't ignore what you can't measure. The intangible elements of your marketing efforts still have value. Focus on passion and authenticity as you sell.

Resources

The full set of resources for this chapter can be found in the Authorpreneur Companion Course. To get the free course and materials, go here:

www.jtev.me/authorpreneur-free-course

Next Steps

This takes us to the end of the 'how to do it' part of the book. In part three, I'll give you the most important takeaways from everything I've learned over the years.

BRI SEELEY

Inspirational women are everywhere, but Bri Seeley has made a career out of it. From her website:

> *Bri is motivated by a deeply-held belief that every woman deserves to live a life that inspires her, and her work reflects this deep remembering that our desires are ultimately inevitable.*

> *Through her signature 6-month training, Permission to Leap (plus best-selling book + podcast by the same name!), she will guide you*

through the process of leaping from the day you commit to your vision, all the way through each stage, up until the day you land softly on the other side of it all.

A catalyst, speaker, and best-selling author, Bri is a regular contributor for The Huffington Post and Influencive and is known around the world for her compassionate, yet tell-it-like-it-is guidance that creates massive and epic changes in every woman she encounters.

My company helped Bri write and launch her book. Throughout the process, we described her as one of our favorite clients because she executed on our teachings relentlessly. *Permission to Leap* became an instant bestseller and racked up nearly 100 reviews in the first week of publication. Bri has been able to use the book as the centerpiece of her brand, and she immediately saw an increase in sales across her business after the launch. In fact, she recouped her investment for our services within the first month of the book's release! She's truly an inspiration, and living proof that when you give yourself permission to leap, you can accomplish amazing things.

Here's Bri's take on it: "I never desired to be an author,

but when *Permission to Leap* came to me and asked to be written—well, I couldn't say no. I went into the process not knowing what authorship could do for me or my brand, and came out of the process as a completely new woman, signing client contracts left and right and possessing not only a marketing tool, but the start of a long-term business strategy that is a seedling for the rest of my career. Becoming a bestselling author was a catalyst for personal and business growth on levels I had only imagined previously."

Want to launch your own book? You can join the free Authorpreneur Companion Course to download our launch materials and learn more about our process.

www.jtev.me/authorpreneur-free-course

PART THREE

BRINGING IT ALL TOGETHER

CHAPTER 9

LESSONS & STRATEGIES

Generating meaningful income from book sales is certainly possible, even without hitting The New York Times Bestseller list. But remember, direct sales is usually not the best approach for gaining maximum leverage from your book in the first place. Books open the door to building a business, launching other products, and being viewed as an expert in your field. Those other areas are where the true value is harvested.

I've spent years writing, launching, and marketing books. I've written two bestsellers that generated over 100,000 sold copies in 24 months. My strategies have helped hundreds of authors launch successfully, and my company has executed over a dozen fully managed launches at the time of this writing, culminating in thousands of book sales, hundreds of reviews, and a 100% hit rate of reaching #1 bestseller status within the first week of publication. It's safe to say I've learned a few things about this industry.

Some Takeaways

1. I spent over $25,000 producing my first book, but most of that cost was unnecessary. You can spend a few thousand dollars and achieve the same, or better, results.

2. More than half of the budget for my first book went to my promo video. I love the video, but it wasn't necessary as a first-time author. If you have a tight budget, skip the promo video.

3. I spent a ton of time writing my book, but very little time writing blog posts, creating my online brand, and building an email list. I should have allocated way more time to the latter, and you should too.

4. The crowdfunding campaign for my first book

was a success in terms of building a list of fans, but it wasn't helpful monetarily. If you use a crowdfunding platform, focus on building a list versus raising funds. Set your funding goal low, and don't spend money on an expensive promo video.

5. Twitter followers are overrated. You should still grow that channel, but place more value on establishing your online brand and building an email list. Read Kevin Kelly's 1,000 True Fans to better understand the importance of having a modest base of super fans versus a massive following on social media.

6. Facebook fans can be valuable if you create a private group and involve them early and often. Using a launch team to amplify your marketing efforts can have a monumental effect on your results.

7. The process of writing and marketing a book can feel overwhelming. It's a good idea to partner with experts who know what they're doing.

8. Design is everything. The market is getting more crowded by the day. A quality design will help you cut through the noise.

9. A final bit of advice: You have to be passionate about your content. If you aren't emotionally engaged and revved up, your readers won't be either. So find something that gets your juices flowing, edit your prose relentlessly, build your brand, and put the time and effort into crafting a base of fans to push you up the rankings when you launch.

Book on a Budget: MED+MVP

Many of the techniques I've mentioned are not critical to your success. Here's the most barebones MED (Minimum Effective Dose) formula that will still give you a perfectly acceptable MVP (Minimum Viable Product) for launch:

1 Write your book.

2 Use Leadpages or ConvertKit to build a landing page to collect early emails.

3 Use Facebook groups to attract early fans and create a launch team.

4 Use a crowdfunding platform to raise some capital.

5 Hire a book designer through Fiverr, 99designs, or a similar service.

6 Launch on Amazon with a digital version and a paperback version (using CreateSpace).

This should all cost less than $2,000 and still provide opportunity for success if your content is good. Remember to involve Facebook friends early and often to build buzz around your launch.

Paid Options

If you *do* have a budget, but feel overwhelmed, there are other options to consider. They come at a cost, but can save you precious time and energy. I've spoken with all of the companies listed below, and worked with a few of them directly as well. Costs can range anywhere from $1,000 to $50,000.

Lifestyle Entrepreneurs Press

http://lifestyleentrepreneurspress.com/

I've personally executed half a dozen launches with Lifestyle Entrepreneurs Press, founded by Jesse Krieger. LEP was one of the ways in which LaunchTeam found its footing. We honed much of our process from doing a handful of initial launches with Jesse Krieger and his team. He's building a hybrid publishing house that takes care of its authors. If you want to work with an innovative partner who understands the new landscape of publishing and how to make the most of it, I'd recommend contacting LEP. Be sure to let them know we sent you!

Book in a Box

www.bookinabox.com

Book in a Box, as I've mentioned, is a publishing company cofounded by Zach Obront and Tucker Max. They're focused on bringing high-quality nonfiction titles to the market using dictation and transcription technology. Combining outlining, interviewing, and speech recording, Book In A Box delivers professionally produced books while only requiring about twelve hours of the author's time.

This approach has been field tested. Tucker and his team have already produced countless successful titles, including *Connect*, by Josh Turner (which hit the Wall Street Journal bestseller list, sold over 10,000 copies, and has amassed over 250 reviews at the time of this writing). The system works particularly well for busy CEO's or celebrities who have a lot of valuable information to share, but don't have the time or interest in sitting down and going through the traditional writing process.

Advantage Publishing

http://advantagefamily.com/

Advantage markets itself as a Business Growth Publisher. They publish business books to help entrepreneurs grow their businesses and/or personal brands.

GreenLeaf

http://www.greenleafbookgroup.com/

Greenleaf focuses on distribution and branding. They have a high quality bar.

Self Publishing School

http://www.self-publishingschool.com/

Chandler Bolt has self-published six #1 bestselling books and runs Self-Publishing School (SPS), a multi-seven-figure business teaching others how to achieve the same success. He's the real deal. I highly recommend SPS if you want to self-publish but can't afford the more expensive services listed above.

TL;DR, Resources, and Next Steps

TL;DR (Summary)

- It's possible to generate meaningful income from book sales, but direct sales is usually not the best way to leverage your book. Instead, use your book to sell other stuff, launch a business, or establish your brand.

- Dedicate time and money to marketing efforts and working with experts to guide you.

- You can launch a book successfully on a budget of a few thousands dollars. The most critical elements are good design and organizing a launch team to amplify your marketing.

- If you want to amp up your success and you have a budget to hire experts, you can work with proven companies who deliver great results, like Lifestyle Entrepreneurs Press, Book in a Box, Advantage, Greenleaf, Self-Publishing School, and others.

Resources

The full set of resources for this chapter can be found in the Authorpreneur Companion Course. To get the free course and materials, go here:

www.jtev.me/authorpreneur-free-course

Next Steps

The next chapter summarizes the entire book. After that, it's time for you to stop reading and start writing. You got this!

STARTUP OPPORTUNITIES

Sean Wise and Brad Feld are venture capitalists. They've seen their fair share of business pitches—more than 30,000 over a span of 20 years. They wrote a book called *Startup Opportunities* that lays out all the common factors for why startups fail, why they succeed, and how to spot the best opportunities when they arise.

On their book's sales page on Amazon, they explain that, "more than five million people will launch a business this year, and many of them will be great ideas—yet few will be around in five years, and even fewer in ten years. A great idea is not enough to build a successful business. You need to fortify your idea with the proper foundation, and a scaffolding of good planning and early action. This book shows you how."[1]

Startup Opportunities was published through a traditional publishing house (Wiley), but we were still able to work with them to employ our launch techniques, which helped the book hit #1 in multiple categories on Amazon. But more importantly, we kept working with Sean and Brad *after* the launch to schedule dozens of appearances on podcasts, radio shows, and across other media outlets like Forbes, Inc., and others. While Sean and Brad are already incredibly successful, the added exposure has had secondary effects that continue to bring them opportunities in relation to the book and beyond.

After going through the process, Dr. Sean Wise said this: "Writing the book is the easy part. Getting people to read it, now that's the trick. Authors today must see the book launch as the start of the journey, not the end."

---

1 https://tinyurl.com/yakbte8b

Want to launch your own book? You can join the free Authorpreneur Companion Course to download our launch materials and learn more about our process.

www.jtev.me/authorpreneur-free-course

CHAPTER 10

TL;DR (IN SUMMARY)

Want the CliffNotes version of this book? Let me break it down for you one more time.

There's never been a better time in history to write a book.

1. Our economy has reached a tipping point that gives individuals leverage over corporations. Entrepreneurship addresses the limit in our society and is now the main source of power. Writing a book is one of the most accessible

first-steps for breaking into entrepreneurship as a skill.

2. As technology continues to democratize the tools of production and distribution, and globalization pushes more jobs overseas, we see a trend of work moving into the creative and complex realms. Writing a nonfiction book capitalizes on this trend, both as a profitable profession, and as a way to feed a growing legion of entrepreneurs.

3. Amazon has accelerated the proliferation of digital content by building the Kindle platform. Their bet on digital books has been a boon for indie authors worldwide. It is now easier and cheaper to distribute books, and the previous barriers to entry have all evaporated. Consumers have also been conditioned to pay for books—even short ones.

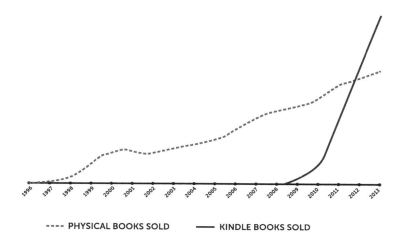

- - - - PHYSICAL BOOKS SOLD ——— KINDLE BOOKS SOLD

There's never been a bigger audience for your book. The market for ebooks is exploding, while the market for physical books is stalling by comparison.[1] This doesn't mean it's a bad time to be a traditionally published author. It just means there are more options.

It's never been easier to write a book.

1. The entrepreneurial community is hungry to learn. Knowledge in *anything*, in the form of a memoir, a technical guide, or a philosophical argument (just to name a few), are in demand like never before.

---

1 https://tinyurl.com/ybkaej9k

2. The internet is everyone's library. A categorically poor person in a remote corner of the world today has better access to knowledge than the wealthiest university student had twenty years ago. Gaining both surface-level *and* deep knowledge in nearly any subject is now possible thanks to the internet and, more specifically, learning platforms like *Teachable, Thinkific, Udemy,* and others.

3. The Long Tail makes hyper-specific content profitable. Writing a book about any topic is more distributable and therefore more profitable today than ever before. Because the internet allows hyper-specific communities to be easily identified and targeted, crafting content for small subsets of society is now a viable business strategy. In fact, the high-value niche market approach has shown it can produce incredibly high returns—into the seven figure range.

4. Software improvements have made writing a book infinitely more feasible, at little or no cost to the writer.
   a. Wikipedia gives us a constantly evolving free encyclopedia for quick research on any topic.

    a. GoogleDocs is a full-featured free word processing software, complete with version control, a built-in dictionary, rich formatting tools, commenting, and the ability to track changes.

    a. Evernote lets us store notes, links, images, and anything else we can find on the web, in a single, organized interface.

    a. Pocket allows us to save full articles and blogs, which can be referenced later.

5. Kindle and CreateSpace give us the tools to launch and distribute both digital and paperback books. No publisher necessary, and no upfront cost.

6. New publishers like Lifestyle Entrepreneurs Press and Book In A Box have come charging onto the scene to help authors who prefer extra care, but don't want to sell their souls to the Big Five publishing houses.

7. Crowdfunding, freelancers, and author platforms such as Publishizer, KickStarter, IndieGogo, LaunchTeam, Winning Edits, Reedsy, Goodreads, Fiverr, and 99Designs have created new ecosystems for building an

audience, raising capital from fans, and hiring contractors to help craft professional-grade products. When done correctly, the quality of self-produced products is indistinguishable from institutional production.

It's never been more profitable to write a book.

1. I earn over five figures directly from my books. This includes sales from the audio versions, and advances from publishing deals in various countries. But more importantly, I've used my experience with book publishing to build a company that helps others find the same success and expands beyond book launches into much, much more. We did six figures in year one.

2. Meng To's first book, *Design+Code* likely generated over seven figures in less than two years (from what I can tell). Meng has also built a company around his product. He now teaches Sketch courses around the world.

3. Nathan Barry earned over six figures from his high-value, niche market books, selling directly to consumers online. He now runs a

multimillion dollar email marketing company called Convertkit, which he self-funded with his book profits.

4. Rob Walling followed a similar path, self-publishing books and then building an email marketing service called Drip. Drip was bought by LeadPages for over a million dollars.

5. Pat Flynn earns well over six figures a year from his latest book, *Will it Fly,* and runs a multimillion dollar business that revolves around the concepts from his book.

6. Chandler Bolt has written six bestsellers, including *Book Launch* and *Published,* which urge people to self-publish books themselves. Based on his success, he launched Self-Publishing School—a set of courses that walks new authors through the process. His annual book sales, combined with the income from Self-Publishing School, hit seven figures after only two years.

I could go on and on. But at some point, I have to stop—and you have to start. Think about this: You could change someone's life with your words. Heck, you could change ten people's lives, or a hundred, or a thousand, or a *million*. You could spark a movement that alters the course of human history. Yes, these are grand statements, but they're not as far-fetched as you might imagine.

Honestly, I can't guarantee you'll change the world or make a million bucks, but I *can* promise you this: *Writing a book will enrich your life.* The principles of writing can be applied to anything you pursue. Are you a musician, an artist, a scientist, a historian, a mathematician, an athlete, an engineer, a student, a mom, or a dad? Are you an entrepreneur of any kind? Do you have experiences that have taught you a lesson? Then you have a book in you. Don't wait for someone to notice you. Don't wait for the college diploma or the job promotion. Start building your own platform *today*. Let your work-ethic, problem-solving skills, and vision transform your dreams into your reality. Use the library in your hand to hone your craft. Hit the *publish* button and share your work with billions of people in an instant.

You're already a member of the most innovative generation this world has ever seen. This isn't just the dawn of books. It's the dawn of an entirely new era. We're entering the Creation Age—the era of the individual, and it's up to you to make the most of it. So tell your story. Build a rich life for yourself. *Become immortal.*

Yes—it's time to write your book.

NEXT STEPS

Get a Free Consultation

Taking your life to the next level requires action, and I can help with that. Want a private consultation with yours truly? I'll consult on whatever you want, in relation to your business or book (content, structure, tone, voice, pacing, Amazon setup, marketing, pricing, launching, etc.), for up to 30 minutes. I would typically charge a good chunk of change for this, but you can get it for free by registering for the *Authorpreneur* Companion Course.

Here's how it works:

1. If you haven't already, join the free Companion Course here: www.jtev.me/authorpreneur-free-course

2. Sit back and relax

That's it. Each month, I randomly select one person from the course to tutor. As long as you follow the steps above, you'll be considered in each monthly drawing.

The 30-Day Authorpreneur Challenge

The biggest speed bump stopping people from completing a project is *a failure to start*. Don't let that be you. Instead, hit the ground running and make yourself accountable. You can do that by joining the *Authorpreneur* Facebook group and taking part in the 30-Day Authorpreneur Challenge. It's simple. Join the group and make a commitment to write content for your book for 30 days in a row. There's no word count requirement—just write *something* each day. Post in the group daily with your current streak (i.e. "Day 1-30"), your word count for that day, and your total word count for the challenge. And feel free to chat with other members of the group for support. You'd be surprised how much it can help. Request to join the private group here:

https://www.facebook.com/groups
/AuthorpreneurGroup/

We'll also be offering other special perks, bonuses, and giveaways within the group. So even if you're not ready to start writing, it's still a good idea to join.

Stay Up-to-Date
This book is a living, breathing resource. I'll be making changes to it as the publishing industry evolves and as I get feedback from readers like you. Join the Companion Course and you'll automatically be notified when any major changes are made.

www.jtev.me/authorpreneur-free-course

Contribute to the Authorpreneur Movement
If you want to contribute to this project, here are a few things you can do:

- *Leave your feedback.* The best way to give feedback is to write a review on Amazon. You can do that by going to Amazon.com and typing "Authorpreneur Jesse Tevelow" in the search bar.

My book will pop up in the results. Click on it, then scroll down the page to the reviews section.

- *Send me your story.* Are you thinking of writing a book? Are you currently writing a book? Have you already launched a book? If you answered "yes" to any of these questions, send me an email describing your experience. If you have an interesting journey, I might feature it in future editions or in our marketing material. Send an email with the subject line: "My Book Story" to jesse. tevelow@gmail.com.

- *Share the book with your friends.* If you really enjoyed this, share it! You have the power to make this book fly. Sharing it on social media or telling a friend can make all the difference in reaching a mainstream audience. I'd be forever grateful to you.

- *Get in touch.* There are a few good ways to reach me directly. The first is my email: jesse.tevelow@ gmail.com. I get a lot of email, so sometimes things slip by. The best option is Twitter. Follow me and tweet @jtevelow. Please also include *#authorpreneur* in your tweet. I try to respond personally to every tweet.

You can always find my latest writings, links to my books, and other updates on my main website: www.jtev.me

Again, if you liked the book, say hi to me on Twitter and let me know. I promise I'll respond. @jtevelow #authorpreneur

BESTSELLER LAUNCH

If you're looking for more guidance, we have a program called the Bulletproof Bestseller Book Launch.

Check it out and see if it's right for you.

http://bit.ly/bulletproof-bestseller

We also offer managed services for select clients. To learn about those, head over to our main website: www.mylaunchteam.com.

ACKNOWLEDGEMENTS

Many, many people helped me write and produce this book. I can't thank them enough. But most of all, I'd like to thank *you*. Support from my readers is what keeps me going.

Now go launch a book and tell me about it so I can check it out. And always remember to...

Keep...
Making...
Moves.

J

ABOUT THE AUTHOR

Jesse Warren Tevelow is a #1 bestselling author, an alumnus of Techstars, and the founder of LaunchTeam. By challenging the world's assumptions, he aims to bring more meaning, freedom, and happiness to people's lives. Jesse has been featured in various publications, including *Bloomberg, Entrepreneur,* and *Forbes,* and appeared on popular podcasts that reach millions of listeners. He lives in sunny Santa Monica, California. To find out more, go to www.jtev.me

Made in the USA
Middletown, DE
09 May 2021